Past Masters
General Editor Keith Thomas

Diderot

Past Masters

AQUINAS Anthony Kenny
ARISTOTLE Jonathan Barnes
FRANCIS BACON Anthony
Quinton
BAYLE Elisabeth Labrousse
BERKELEY J. O. Urmson
THE BUDDHA Michael Carrithers
BURKE C. B. Macpherson
CARLYLE A. L. Le Quesne
CLAUSEWITZ Michael Howard
COBBETT Raymond Williams
COLERIDGE Richard Holmes
CONFUCIUS Raymond Dawson
DANTE George Holmes
DARWIN Jonathan Howard
DIDEROT Peter France
GEORGE ELIOT Rosemary
Ashton

ENGELS Terrell Carver
GALILEO Stillman Drake
HEGEL Peter Singer
HOMER Jasper Griffin
HUME A. J. Ayer
JESUS Humphrey Carpenter
KANT Roger Scruton
MACHIAVELLI Quentin Skinner
MARX Peter Singer
MONTAIGNE Peter Burke
THOMAS MORE Anthony Kenny
WILLIAM MORRIS Peter Stansky
MUHAMMAD Michael Cook
NEWMAN Owen Chadwick
PASCAL Alban Krailsheimer
PLATO R. M. Hare
PROUST Derwent May
TOLSTOY Henry Gifford

Forthcoming

AUGUSTINE Henry Chadwick
BACH Denis Arnold
BERGSON Leszek Kolakowski
JOSEPH BUTLER R. G. Frey
CERVANTES P. E. Russell
CHAUCER George Kane
COPERNICUS Owen Gingerich
ERASMUS James McConica
GIBBON J. W. Burrow
GODWIN Alan Ryan
GOETHE T. J. Reed
HERZEN Aileen Kelly
JEFFERSON Jack P. Greene
JOHNSON Pat Rogers
LAMARCK L. J. Jordanova

LEIBNIZ G. M. Ross
LINNAEUS W. T. Stearn
LOCKE John Dunn
MENDEL Vitezslav Orel
MILL William Thomas
NEWTON P. M. Rattansi
ST PAUL G. B. Caird
PETRARCH Nicholas Mann
RUSKIN George P. Landow
SHAKESPEARE Germaine Greer
ADAM SMITH D. D. Raphael
SOCRATES Bernard Williams
SPINOZA Roger Scruton
VICO Peter Burke
and others

Peter France

Diderot

Oxford New York

OXFORD UNIVERSITY PRESS

1983

Oxford University Press, Walton Street, Oxford OX2 6DP

London Glasgow New York Toronto
Delhi Bombay Calcutta Madras Karachi
Kuala Lumpur Singapore Hong Kong Tokyo
Nairobi Dar es Salaam Cape Town
Melbourne Auckland

and associates in
Beirut Berlin Ibadan Mexico City Nicosia

British Library Cataloguing in Publication Data

France, Peter, 1935 –
Diderot – (Past masters)
1. Diderot, Denis – Criticism and interpretation
I. Title II. Series
194 B2017
ISBN 0-19-287551-5
ISBN 0-19-287550-7 Pbk

Set by Colset Pte Ltd, Singapore
Printed in Great Britain by
William Clowes (Beccles) Ltd
Beccles and London

Preface

Diderot is not as well known to British readers as he deserves to be. Regrettably few of his books are easily available in translation. In this essay I have tried to show something of the richness and interest of his thought and writing, in the hope that this will bring him more readers and perhaps even encourage the publication of more translations.

I have been reading, studying, translating and discussing Diderot on and off for over fifteen years. Inevitably therefore my views have been influenced in ways which I cannot fully trace by the views of friends, colleagues and students; I am grateful to them all. I also owe a great deal to the scholars and critics who have written so well about Diderot; some of their work is indicated in the 'Further reading' section. And my particular thanks go to John Hope Mason, John Renwick, Siân Reynolds and Anthony Strugnell, who have read drafts of this book and helped me with their comments.

Edinburgh   PETER FRANCE

Contents

Note on texts and abbreviations

All translations in the following pages are my own. Since the new complete edition of Diderot's works is at the time of writing some way from completion, I have referred where possible to the readily available volumes in the Classiques Garnier collection:

E   *Œuvres esthétiques* (ed. P. Vernière, Paris, 1959)

P   *Œuvres politiques* (ed. P. Vernière, Paris, 1963)

PH *Œuvres philosophiques* (ed. P. Vernière, Paris, 1956)

R   *Œuvres romanesques* (ed. H. Bénac, revised by L. Perol, Paris, 1981)

Other references are to the following editions:

A   *Œuvres complètes* (ed. J. Assézat and M. Tourneux, Paris, 1875–77), 20 vols

O   *Oeuvres complètes* (edited under the direction of H. Dieckmann, J. Proust and J. Varloot, Paris, 1975–), 13 vols to date

C   *Correspondance* (ed. G. Roth and J. Varloot, Paris, 1955–70), 16 vols

PD *Pensées détachées, contributions à l'Histoire des deux Indes* (ed. G. Goggi, Siena, 1976)

1 A master?

A few years before his death, Denis Diderot, who was no poet, wrote a self-portrait in verse which ends like this:

> When on my sarcophagus
> Pallas Athene, all in tears,
> Points to these words engraved in stone:
> 'Here lies a wise man', do not laugh
> And indiscreetly give the lie
> To sad Minerva, do not shame
> My honoured memory with the words:
> 'Here lies a fool' . . . keep it to yourself. (A IX 57)

Like not a few 'past masters' (including two of his own favourites, Socrates and Montaigne), Diderot was not entirely at ease in the role of public mentor. In his lifetime he hid his light under many bushels and had few disciples. Nor indeed has he had many since. We are familiar with Voltaireans and Rousseauists, but there are no Diderotians or Diderotists. His two great contemporaries were stars in their own day, and their deaths were European events. They gained a head start over him, and they have never lost that lead. For most of his contemporaries, Diderot was the editor of an encyclopedia rather than what he has become for us, an author of major books. Much of his best work was published only after his death, and over the last two hundred years he has tended to be a writer for the happy few. He inspired Goethe and Schiller, he was Marx's favourite prose writer (if we are to believe a Victorian domestic questionnaire), but he has scarcely become a household name, even in France. He deserves to be much better known.

Nevertheless, Diderot has continued, directly or indirectly, to provoke and even to scandalise not only such nineteenth-century readers as Carlyle or Émile Faguet, but also the censor of the film by Jacques Rivette based on his novel *The Nun*, banned in France in 1965. Others have been inspired and excited by him, and even if he has not been the fountainhead of any school, he has generated the contradictory readings which are the posthumous lot of great writers.

The clearest line of interpretation, from the eighteenth century to the present, has been the radical tradition. In the first edition of his works, published by the atheist Naigeon, he appears as a subversive yet respectable philosopher, a rational enemy of superstition and despotism. A similar image is implicit in the Third Republic edition of his writings by Assézat and Tourneux. The enthusiasm of Hegel, Marx and Engels has helped him to a place in the socialist canon. In the nineteenth century some of his writings were serialised in left-wing newspapers, and more recently his books have figured prominently in the French Communist Party's collection of People's Classics. In the Soviet Union too he has been adopted as a great ancestor – one moreover who actually went to Russia and whose manuscripts are still preserved in the former capital of Catherine the Great.

The radical line in the interpretation of Diderot has been powerful, but it has several rivals. For some latter-day Romantics he was (and is) a force of nature and the precursor of a new aesthetic. Liberals have been glad to observe his open-minded humanism. He has been called a 'happy existentialist'. And recent commentators, taking a more literary view of him, have been drawn to the ironic, fragmented and polyphonic quality of his writing, which prefigures – or so it is claimed – a certain kind of modernism. All of these approaches highlight his openness, his willingness to welcome variety and to engage in dialogue.

What we can for convenience call the radical and the liberal views of Diderot, stressing respectively his militant message and his protean pluralism, point to an important tension in his work which will be close to the centre of this book. Explicitly or implicitly I shall be asking whether it is a set of ideas that matters most in Diderot, or else a characteristic stance, a way of being and a way of writing. I shall be looking at the interplay in his work between teaching and learning, monologues and dialogue, the one and the many. What sort of a master was he?

Like all writers, Diderot changed as he grew older, but he returned constantly to the same questions, ideas and images, and remained faithful to the same impulses. Rather than structure this short book round his historical development, I thought it best therefore, after an introductory chapter which provides a chronological framework for what follows, to concentrate on some of these constants in his work. And rather than study separately and successively his ideas on different subjects (science, politics, art, ethics, etc.), I have preferred to dwell on some of the fundamental aspects of his writing and thinking which cut across all the chronological divisions and all the different kinds of subject-matter to which he addressed himself. But first it is necessary to have an idea of his career and the world he lived in.

2 Life, family, society

Diderot was very much a Frenchman; for all his interest in other countries and cultures, he spent almost all his life either in his birth-place, Langres, some 150 miles south-east of Paris, or in the capital and its immediate surroundings. Only after he had reached the age of sixty did he make the one long journey of his life, to Holland and Russia; only then did he see the sea for the first time.

He was born in 1713, two years before the death of Louis XIV. He was to live most of his life under the long and generally peaceful reign of Louis XV, a period of growing prosperity, in which France took her first slow steps on the road of modernisation. It was still a traditional society, dominated by the old élites, a rural society in which some four-fifths of French people lived on the land, many of them unable to read or write. But it was also a time of colonial expansion, of commercial and industrial development; in the eyes of Diderot's contemporaries, money and business were attaining a new importance in French society. It is a historian's joke that wherever you look in early modern Europe the bourgeoisie is always rising and the peasants are always revolting, but certainly in eighteenth-century France the commercial and professional classes enjoyed a higher status than before, and the practical values which are often (perhaps misleadingly) associated with the bourgeoisie were in the ascendant. In this movement, which is a part of what is meant by the term 'Enlightenment', Denis Diderot played a leading role.

It is important always to bear in mind that Diderot's background was solidly provincial. His father was a cutler, a propertied artisan who was wealthy enough to leave an estate of some 100,000 *livres* – at a time when it was estimated that the average annual consumption among peasants in a backward region was the equivalent of some 35 *livres* per head. The family circle in Langres figures prominently in Diderot's letters, and he depicts it vividly in an entertaining dialogue of 1771 called *Conversation of a Father with his Children*. To judge from these writings, his father was a dominating figure in Diderot's life. The two did not always live in harmony (as when the father tried to prevent his son's marriage by having him held in custody in a monastery), but the old cutler came to be for Diderot an incarnation of the most precious social virtues – benevolence, integrity, family affection. In 1770 he recalled sentimentally how pleased he had been when, some years after his father's death, a Langres man had said to him: 'You are a good man, Monsieur Diderot; but if you think you will ever be your father's equal, you are wrong' (A XVII 335). It seems likely that in his own public and quite genuine enthusiasm for virtue, and in his own conduct as a father, Diderot was trying to live up to this example of excellence.

Of Diderot's mother we know very little, except that she died in 1748 and that he remembered her with affection. His younger brother and his sisters stand out in sharper relief. His brother became a priest; the philosopher saw him as unbending and intolerant, a living example of the bad effect of religious belief on a decent human being. Of his two sisters who survived childhood, one apparently died mad in a convent (this is echoed in Diderot's novel *The Nun*), whereas the other was more like her elder brother – 'a kind of female Diogenes', in his words. Denis was the only one who moved away from Langres, and even he, while becoming Parisian,

5

retained close ties with his provincial homeland and eventually married his daughter to a young man from Langres. In 1752 he wrote to a compatriot, using the local dialect, that he would always be 'Deniseu Didereut, son of master Didier Didereut, cutler at the sign of the pearl in Langres' (C I 142).

In a letter of 1760, Diderot recalled as one of the happiest days of his life the occasion when he arrived home from school laden with prizes, to be greeted by his father weeping tears of joy (C III 157). For clever young provincials, education was the key to social advancement – though it did not take Denis quite where his father had intended. Like many French writers of his century, he attended the local Jesuit college and at the age of about fifteen went on to continue his studies in the capital, where he graduated as Master of Arts in 1732. There is some uncertainty about the schools he attended in Paris, but one can say with confidence that his early education at least was dominated by rhetoric and the study of the classics. Unlike most of his contemporaries, Diderot knew some Greek, and such Latin and Greek writers as Horace, Lucretius, Plutarch and Plato were always close to his heart, even when his speculations and scientific interests led him into very advanced areas. As for rhetoric, the art of speech, it doubtless helped him to develop his own gifts as speaker and writer, his taste for arguing both sides of a question and his love of the eloquent set piece.

The young master of arts was supposed to become a lawyer; instead, to his father's dismay, he embarked on the risky career of man of letters and eventually *philosophe* (a term which in its eighteenth-century meaning is close to the modern 'intellectual'). His first steps on this road remain obscure; he seems to have led a life of temporary expedients, which is perhaps reflected in one of his greatest works, *Rameau's Nephew* (*Le Neveu de Rameau*). In 1742 he married

6

the poor but beautiful Antoinette Champion, secretly and against his father's wishes. The couple had several children, of whom only one reached adult years – Angélique, born in 1753, the object of great paternal affection. As for Madame Diderot, to judge from the words of those who knew her (not least her husband), she was, or became, a difficult person to live with. This was no doubt caused or exacerbated by her husband's neglect; in his married life he was no model of traditional virtue, but he remained loyal to her in his own way and from time to time tried to make amends.

By the 1740s Diderot was beginning to gain a reputation and to make friends and allies in the world of letters. Those close to him included Jean-Jacques Rousseau, who had come to Paris to make his fortune with a new system of musical notation; the philosopher Condillac, who in 1746 published his *Essay on the Origin of Human Knowledge* (*Essai sur l'origine des connaissances humaines*); the mathematician and scientist d'Alembert, and the German Melchior Grimm, a journalist and man of letters who was to remain an intimate friend almost to the end. To keep himself alive, Diderot engaged in various forms of literary work, above all translation. His first significant work was a heavily annotated version of the English philosopher Shaftesbury's *Inquiry concerning Merit and Virtue*, preceded by an open letter to his brother which is a critique of religious intolerance.

Even more important for his career was the plan to publish a French version of Ephraim Chambers's *Cyclopedia*. In 1746 Diderot was appointed – with d'Alembert – general editor of this work; it was to occupy an immense part of his life for the next twenty years. The planned translation quickly grew into an original work, which in the end amounted to seventeen folio volumes of text and a further twelve of plates. The history of its publication was stormy. From the beginning it

7

had powerful enemies as well as powerful protectors. There were skirmishes in the early 1750s, principally with the Jesuits, but the real blow fell half-way through publication, in 1759, when the Parlement of Paris outlawed the work. This was not the end, however; thanks to the connivance of the authorities, the remaining volumes were eventually issued unofficially in Paris. In spite or because of persecution, the *Encyclopedia* was a huge success. The list of subscribers kept growing, and a whole series of cheaper editions quickly followed. It was a major commercial undertaking, providing work and income for many people, including Diderot himself, who was one of the first French writers to make a living principally by his literary earnings.

To his contemporaries he was above all the editor of the *Encyclopedia*. For years it kept him busy, at times it was a millstone round his neck. It is true that d'Alembert was responsible for the famous *Preliminary Discourse* and many important articles, but he backed out when there was trouble, and in any case Diderot did most of the real work of general editor, chasing up contributors, rewriting their articles and writing a huge number himself. All of this, wearing as it might be, was very valuable to him; the *Encyclopedia* gave him a vantage point on French society, putting him in touch with many different aspects of the world he lived in, and with men and women of all kinds, from the very eminent (Montesquieu, Voltaire) to the artisans from whom he elicited details of their craft.

The troubles of 1758–9 were not Diderot's first brush with authority. In 1747 he had been denounced to the Lieutenant General of Police as 'a very dangerous man who speaks with contempt of the holy mysteries of religion' (C I 54). His first significant works, which include *Philosophical Thoughts (Pensées philosophiques*, 1746), *The Sceptic's Walk*

(*La Promenade du sceptique*, 1747) and *Letter on the Blind* (*Lettre sur les aveugles*, 1749) together with the licentious novel *The Indiscreet Jewels* (*Les Bijoux indiscrets*, 1748) were all unorthodox in one way or another. All of them were either published anonymously or (in the case of *The Sceptic's Walk*) left unpublished in their author's lifetime. In 1749, in a government crackdown on subversive writing, Diderot was imprisoned in the Chateau of Vincennes. He was only set free when he had promised 'to do nothing in future which is in any way contrary to religion or morality' (C I 96). His stay at Vincennes was not very prolonged (about a hundred days), but it alarmed him; this is one reason why he subsequently adopted roundabout ways of expressing himself and left much of his best work unpublished.

In the 1750s most of his efforts as a writer were devoted to the *Encyclopedia*, but he also produced two philosophical works, a *Letter on the Deaf and Dumb* (*Lettre sur les sourds et muets*, 1752) and the *Thoughts on the Interpretation of Nature* (*Pensées sur l'interprétation de la nature*, 1753). Then, in the second half of the decade, he became a dramatist and a dramatic theorist. The theatre occupied a central place in French cultural life, and Diderot had long been interested in it. This interest led in the 1750s to a vigorous campaign for the reform of the Parisian stage. The result was two plays, *The Natural Son* (*Le Fils naturel*, 1757) and *The Father* (*Le Père de famille*, 1758) and two theoretical works, *Conversations about 'The Natural Son'* (*Entretiens sur le Fils Naturel*, 1757) and the *Discourse on Dramatic Poetry* (*Discours sur la poésie dramatique*, 1758). The *philosophe* did not have a great deal of theatrical experience, and his plays were not an unqualified success, but his innovatory ideas about the theatre were to bear fruit all over Europe in the years to come.

As playwright and *encyclopédiste*, Diderot was in the public

9

eye in the 1750s. He was perceived by his contemporaries as a *philosophe*, a member of the party of radical intellectuals. At the end of this decade, after the outbreak of the Seven Years War and Damiens's attempt on the King's life, this party came under determined attack from several quarters – the Church, the Jesuits, the Parlements, a powerful clique at court, and hostile groups of writers. Diderot himself was vilified and ridiculed, notably in Palissot's play *Les Philosophes*, where he appeared as a bombastic and villainous charlatan. Such assaults, coupled with the banning of the *Encyclopedia*, made this a black period for him, and various factors in his private life made things worse.

In the first place there was the quarrel with his close friend Rousseau. In 1756, in a self-conscious break with Parisian life and with many of the values of the *philosophes*, Jean-Jacques had gone to live in the country; his relations with Diderot became increasingly strained and in 1758 came a break which left indelible marks in the minds of both men. The rights and wrongs of the quarrel will never be established to everyone's satisfaction, but Diderot for his part came to regard Rousseau as a scoundrel, especially after the publication of the *Confessions*; in one of his last works he describes him as a 'monster', an 'atrocious man who does not hesitate to slander his former friends', 'a wicked man who is cunning enough to give credibility to the horrors he tells about others by confessing horrors on his own account' (A III 91–100). For all this, his old friend was to remain a vital point of reference for him; his works are best understood when they are seen alongside Rousseau's.

At the same time his domestic life was far from happy. His marriage had not brought him much satisfaction for many years, but in 1755 he fell in love with Sophie Volland, an unmarried woman three years younger than himself. Sophie was jealously guarded by a mother who took her off to their country home for long spells. To this enforced separation we owe a marvellous sequence of love letters, which are also the nearest Diderot ever came to writing an autobiography. Sophie brought him inspiration and happiness, but also frustration – and domestic storms from the understandably embittered Madame Diderot. In some of his letters of this period, and implicitly in such works as *The Nun* (*La Religieuse*, 1760) and *Rameau's Nephew* (begun in 1761) there is a dark strain which belies the impression of cheerful and active sociability given by so much of his writing.

In the 1760s Sophie was the person nearest to Diderot's heart. He also saw a great deal of various Parisian men of letters, artists and *philosophes*, notably in the circle of the baron d'Holbach, a militant atheist who was rich and hospitable. Diderot spent long periods in d'Holbach's country house just outside Paris, and he was also sometimes the guest of Madame d'Épinay, Rousseau's former protector and the mistress of Grimm, who, with Sophie, represented his ideal audience at this time. Grimm played an important part in Diderot's career as a writer. He was the editor of the *Correspondance littéraire*, a manuscript newsletter which was circulated to a small number of rich and powerful subscribers throughout Europe. This was to be an invaluable semi-private outlet for Diderot's writings for the rest of his life; as well as many short essays and reviews, most of his best work from 1759 onwards appeared first of all in the *Correspondance*. The tyrannical Grimm, badgering his friend for copy, often provided the stimulus he needed to write. In particular, beginning in 1759, he provided Grimm with accounts of the biennial *Salons* of the Academy of Painting and Sculpture, which are among the earliest examples of modern art criticism.

Apart from the rich and exuberant *Salons* and the associated *Essays on Painting* (*Essais sur la peinture*, 1766), the

11

1760s were not a prolific time for Diderot. His work on the *Encyclopedia* dragged on until 1765. In the early 1760s it seems likely that he wrote most of *Rameau's Nephew*. Otherwise there was no major piece of writing until a new creative outburst began in 1769 with *D'Alembert's Dream* (*Le Rêve de d'Alembert*). One of his main concerns during this decade was for his daughter's future. His father had died in 1759, and it was his turn to play the role of *paterfamilias* which he had embodied in the more successful of his two plays. His share of his father's estate brought an increase in income, but even so he was much preoccupied by the need to give Angélique a decent dowry. It was with this in mind that in 1765 he sold his library to Catherine the Great of Russia. 'Sold' is a misnomer, since he was left the use of his books during his lifetime, and it was only after his death that both books and manuscripts were sent to St Petersburg. Effectively this meant that Diderot was being pensioned by a despot, albeit an enlightened one.

Eventually, in June 1773, his debt of gratitude to Catherine led him to embark on the one long journey of his life, a journey which took him first to Holland, where he spent the summer, and then to St Petersburg. He stayed five months in the Russian capital, then returned to the Hague and finally arrived home in the autumn of 1774. It was a long and hazardous journey for a man of sixty who had once declared: 'Personally I do not approve of people going abroad except between the ages of eighteen and twenty-one' (C III 131). One may be reminded of the elderly Dr Johnson setting out into the wilds of Scotland. Like Johnson, Diderot was an observant traveller with an eye to political and social realities. He was not able to see a great deal of Russia from the capital, the more so since he did not know the language, but his visit did bring him into close contact with a powerful monarch. He met Catherine regularly for two or three hours at a time, and

Grimm wrote of these conversations to a correspondent: 'With her he is just as odd, just as original, just as much Diderot as when he is with you. He takes her hand as he takes yours, he sits down by her side as he sits down by yours . . .' (C XIII 111). It is doubtful whether he had any real influence on the actual policies of his patron; she distrusted his idealism and he, while impressed by her personality, later confided to Madame Necker: 'Our *philosophes*, who give the impression of best having known what despotism is, have seen it only through the neck of a bottle. What a difference there is between a tiger painted by Oudry and a tiger in the forest!' (C XIV 72–3).

Certainly the visit to Russia prompted a great increase in his political writing – notably the reflections published as *Notes for Catherine II* (*Mémoires pour Catherine II*, 1773) and the *Observations on the Nakaz* (*Observations sur le Nakaz*, 1774). But even before this visit Diderot had interested himself in political and economic questions. In 1770 he published an *Apology for Abbé Galiani* (*Apologie de l'abbé Galiani*) to defend the theories of his Neapolitan friend against the fashionable doctrines of the Physiocrats, proponents of the unrestricted freedom of the grain trade. Even more important, throughout the 1770s he contributed at great length (and anonymously) to abbé Raynal's *History of the Two Indies* (*Histoire des deux Indes*), a vast and sometimes radical compilation devoted to Europe's colonial expansion. It is hard to be sure exactly what he wrote for Raynal, but this work must certainly be set alongside the *Encyclopedia* and the *Correspondance littéraire* as a major outlet for his writing.

Apart from these political concerns, the 1770s were a fruitful time for Diderot the writer, particularly the five years from 1769 to 1774. As well as *D'Alembert's Dream*, he composed or began at this time a series of major works, including a number of short stories and dialogues, the *Supplement to Bougainville's*

Voyage (*Supplément au Voyage de Bougainville*, 1772), important commentaries on philosophical works by Helvétius and Hemsterhuis, the *Elements of Physiology* (*Eléments de physiologie*), the novel (or anti-novel) *Jacques the Fatalist* (*Jacques le fataliste*, begun around 1771), the *Paradox of the Actor* (*Paradoxe sur le comédien*, 1773) and two further *Salons*. Almost all these remained unpublished in book form, but this does not mean that he was careless about their fate. He had always set great store by the verdict of posterity – the unbeliever's version of immortality – defending this concern against his cynical sculptor friend, Falconet, in an exchange of letters of 1765–7. In the last years of his life he devoted a lot of attention to preparing his writings for eventual publication, so that after his death fair copies of almost all his works could be sent off to St Petersburg (where they still remain).

In the words of his biographer, Arthur Wilson, 'Diderot's life in the decade after his return from Saint Petersburg seems muted and crepuscular'. His family life had settled down, his daughter had married in 1772, and his relation with Sophie (which had been interrupted in 1770 by a last passionate affair with Madame de Maux) had become a tranquil friendship. He was by now a famous old man, receiving recognition from as far away as Edinburgh. He continued to contribute to Raynal's *History*, to revise and add to his earlier works, and to write new ones, the most important being the *Plan of a University for Russia* (*Plan d'une université pour le gouvernement de Russie*, 1775), a play called *Is he good? Is he bad?* (*Est-il bon? Est-il méchant?*, 1781) and his swansong, the semi-autobiographical *Essay on the Reigns of Claudius and Nero* (*Essai sur les règnes de Claude et de Néron*, 1782). His final year was spent in constant ill-health and he died in July 1784, at the age of seventy, a few months after Sophie Volland.

When we consider his life as a whole, Diderot appears as the exemplary *philosophe*, a man who lived for writing, talk and the exchange and pursuit of ideas. In his century the man of letters was beginning to enjoy a new status in society; no longer a mere entertainer or a detached observer, he could aspire to become an 'unacknowledged legislator', a benefactor of humanity. Diderot is always very conscious of this new role and of the difficulty of sustaining it. In particular he returns frequently to the importance of intellectual freedom and economic independence. These were imperilled by the need to ensure a safe passage for his writing, but above all by the need for financial support. Although he received money and eventually an inheritance from his provincial family, he was hardly in the position of Montesquieu or Buffon, who could rely on their private means. He had to have a source of income, and this meant patronage, a sinecure, or living by the pen. The question of independence is central to his key work, *Rameau's Nephew*, which shows (among many other things) a Diderot who is driven by the corruption of his society to imagine himself briefly in the role of the cynic philosopher Diogenes, repudiating Paris and living off roots and water, rather than prostituting himself to the rich and powerful.

This was only a fantasy. In reality, with the need to provide his daughter's dowry and a fair love of creature comforts such as good food, Diderot never played the part of Diogenes, nor indeed that of Socrates, who died in the cause of truth. However, his uneasiness at his position in society persisted to the end of his life. The *Essay on the Reigns of Claudius and Nero* is a protracted defence of the anti-Rousseau, the philosopher who lives in the world, at the court of the despot, sacrificing his moral purity to the good of humanity. Similarly, *Is he good? Is he bad?* portrays a character very like the author, engaged in all kinds of underhand, if beneficial, activities.

15

Can the master also be a rogue? Diderot's trajectory as a thinker led through science, art, music, politics and much else besides, but it would not be an exaggeration to see this wrestling over questions of vice and virtue as the point on which his various explorations converge.

3 Diderot the writer

Whether or not Diderot was a 'master', he wrote no obvious masterpiece, no great novel like *The Brothers Karamazov*, no central philosophical treatise such as the *Essay on Human Understanding*, no systematic body of work such as that of Descartes or Hegel. If he can be associated with any single large-scale enterprise, it must be the *Encyclopedia*, but here, though he was the prime mover, his own contributions are embedded in a mass of other writing, so much so that it is misleading to extract them and present them in the context of his complete works. Although his writings can be (and have been) gathered together in monumental editions, they are scattered in many places, and many of the best of them are couched in forms which lie outside the mainstream of literary production – commentaries, letters, articles, dialogues and the like. As against Montesquieu, who devoted the last twenty years of his life to his own master work, *The Spirit of the Laws* (*De l'esprit des lois*, 1748) and finished his preface with Correggio's proud boast, 'I too am a painter', Diderot was conscious – sometimes ruefully so – that he let his abundant energies flow along unpredictable channels, responding to the stimulus of the moment, the appeals of publishers, friends and acquaintances, the promptings of the books, events and people he met with in his daily life.

A central feature of his writing is that he likes to start from what Jean Starobinski has called 'the word of the other'. This is to say that his words will entwine themselves round some existing text, engulfing it, transforming it, arguing with it and often making it into something quite new and unexpected.

This happens most obviously with translation. The early rendering of Shaftesbury's *Inquiry*, while remaining tolerably faithful to the original, is still Diderot's own work, not only because of the prefatory letter and the numerous footnotes, but because as he worked he digested Shaftesbury, and in so doing laid down many of the principles and posed many of the questions which were to last him for the rest of his life.

The *Encyclopedia* too began life as a parasitic enterprise – here again we can see how translation gave rise to a new creation. Throughout Diderot's work we can see how his thinking and writing are nourished by the presence of earlier writers: the classics, Bacon, Montaigne, Richardson and many more. Of course he is not unusual in borrowing heavily from predecessors; what is rather less normal is that so much of his writing is openly presented as an extension of other people's. A parallel case might be Montaigne, whose *Essays* are built around meditations on quotations from classical authors. At all events, time and again we find Diderot using another text as a jumping-off point. Writers who sent him their manuscripts were liable to have them altered beyond recognition; painters were told in the *Salons* how they should really have composed their canvases. As for his own works, the *Supplement to Bougainville's Voyage* is, as its name implies, a fictitious addition to an existing work; the *Conversations about 'The Natural Son'* present his ideas about the theatre in the guise of a commentary on a supposed production of one of his own plays; *The Nun* is a novel invented on the basis of an exchange of real letters which was in fact a practical joke; and some of his most interesting work, such as the *Refutation of Helvétius* (*Réfutation d'Helvétius*) and the *Commentary on Hemsterhuis* (*Commentaire sur Hemsterhuis*), takes the form of annotations of printed texts.

In all this one notices not only the absorption of other people's words and ideas, but a strong tendency to deception and hoaxing. Most of Diderot's dramatic and fictional works play games with reality, defying the reader to disentangle the actual from the invented. The *Supplement* offers a fine example of this process. It begins with a conversation between 'A' and 'B', who are strolling in the gardens of a country house, discussing the recently published *Voyage round the World* of the French explorer Bougainville. After a few exchanges (which are really a book review in dialogue form), 'B' shows 'A' what is claimed to be an unpublished section of the *Voyage*. It concerns Bougainville's stay in Tahiti and begins with an eloquent speech by an old man who denounces the evils which colonial expansion brings to innocent islanders. The cue for this scene is indeed to be found in a passage where Bougainville mentions a 'venerable' old man, but the 'Old Man's Farewell' is entirely Diderot's invention; it is followed by a teasingly self-conscious passage where 'A', while admiring the speech, remarks that 'through its abrupt and savage tone I think I can see European ideas and ways of talking', and 'B' explains that it is a translation from Tahitian into Spanish and then into French (PH 472–3).

Diderot's readers have to keep their wits about them; they must be alive to shifts of tone and ironical juxtapositions. While it would be wrong to credit him with a radical modernist distrust of writing and indeed of language itself, one of his virtues is certainly a strong degree of self-awareness as a writer. Many of his books, from the *Letter on the Deaf and Dumb* to *Rameau's Nephew*, show that he was conscious of the unreliability of language as a medium for communication. Similarly he knew how viewpoint can distort our vision, and how we use words for deceit and disguise. This is very apparent in his fiction, which is full of reflections on the ways in which one person can persuade another; Diderot places story

19

within story, interrupting these by the remarks and questions of supposed listeners so that the reader is constantly reminded that what he is reading is not the unmediated truth. In his more philosophical writing too, he will characteristically drop his philosophical stance for an ironic or playful aside. *D'Alembert's Dream*, for instance, which concerns such serious issues as the nature of human thought-processes, is full of flippant passages. Thus at one point one of the interlocutors, Mademoiselle de Lespinasse, who at this stage in the dialogue represents the frivolous reader, interrupts the flow of the exposition to ask why philosophers do not all use the charming comparisons which are to be found in the writings of Fontenelle. When Bordeu, the scientist of the piece, replies that such frills are not suitable for such grave questions, she retorts: 'I call them follies; I can allow people to dream about them when they are asleep, but a sensible person will never concern himself with them in his waking hours' (PH 305). In fact the mad dreams spill over on to waking sobriety, and the lady too is caught up by them. The mockery does not cancel out the seriousness of what precedes and follows it, but it calls on us to move quickly from one attitude to another, following the text wherever it leads.

It is not surprising that Diderot set great store by conversation. He himself was a powerful talker, to judge for instance from the *Memoirs* of Marmontel (ed. J. Renwick, I 226). For him, as for Rousseau, speech was superior to writing: his narrator in *The Sceptic's Walk*, presenting the supposed record of a conversation, declares: 'I do not doubt that in being written down, these things have lost much of the energy and life they possessed when spoken' (O II 77). The preamble to the *Conversations about 'The Natural Son'* goes one stage further:

What a difference between what Dorval said to me and what I write . . . I can no longer see Dorval; I can no longer hear him. I am alone amidst the dust of books in the obscurity of a study . . . and I write lines that are weak, sad and cold. (E 79)

Conversation has the advantage of the living presence, and it must be the writer's aim, through his eloquence, to recover some of the strength and warmth that has been lost. But there is more to it than this. Writing tends to impose a constricting order on the free flow of speech; the author is compelled to limit himself, to commit himself too fully to one particular line of thought. 'A book is a great obstacle to truth for an author', wrote Diderot to the Dutch philosopher Hemsterhuis. By contrast, conversation, with its unpredictable twists and turns, allows for a much more exploratory approach:

It's a strange business, conversation, especially when there are several people involved. Just look at the circuitous routes we have followed. The dreams of a sick person in a delirium are not more variegated. Yet just as there is nothing disconnected in the mind of a dreamer or a madman, so everything hangs together in conversation. (C III 172–3)

Everything hangs together – for what Diderot is after is not complete disorder but the subtler order which gives a more adequate expression to the complexity of experience. And there is no doubt that in many of his works he attempted to preserve or imitate this creative order. 'I am not composing, I am not an author; I am reading or conversing, questioning or answering', he declares at the outset of the *Essay on the Reigns of Claudius and Nero* (A III 10), and again and again he claims the right to digress, to emancipate himself from the strict order of logical proceeding, to follow instead the logic of chance association, imaginative analogy and dreaming. Perhaps the neatest and most persuasive of such pleas in the fable of the cuckoo and the nightingale, which he told to Sophie

Volland in a letter of 1760 (C III 166–9). It is an old fable: the cuckoo and the nightingale argue about the respective merits of their songs; they ask for the judgement of a donkey, and he, having listened with his big ears to their characteristic per- formances, declares in favour of the cuckoo's regularity, as against the 'bizarre, confused, disjointed' performance of the nightingale. Diderot was a nightingale, and there have been many cuckoos and donkeys who have reproached him with it. Not all of his writing is chaotic by any means, but to get the best out of it we must abandon the desire for the well-ordered, unified piece of writing. Though there may well be a deeper unity in his works, it will not usually be handed to the reader on a plate.

Conversation is characterised not only by its looser order, but by its multiplicity of voices. By contrast, what we usually think of as a book is the transcription of a single voice, a discourse or a story uttered by a single speaker. The speaker, narrator or author may allow others to speak, but his or her voice will dominate the book. Of course, there are many exceptions to this – the printed play being the most obvious – and in recent years much has been made of the Russian critic Bakhtin's notion of 'polyphony', especially in the novel. In the eighteenth century there were certain genres which gave institutional existence to this polyphony, notably the novel in letter form and the dialogue. For all his admiration of Richardson, Diderot did not imitate his novels, but he is pre-eminently the man of dialogue, and arguably the only exponent of the form who can stand alongside Plato. He wrote dialogues on all sorts of subjects, from music teaching to biology, from acting technique to sexual morality, and he wrote many different kinds of dialogue. There are those (such as the *Paradox of the Actor*) where the form is primarily an aid to persuasive exposition and the conversational devices seem unrealistic or perfunctory, like the 'Yes, Socrates' of some of the Platonic dialogues. There are others, however, in which the dialogue is truly dramatic, an interplay of personalities as well as an exchange of ideas. *Rameau's Nephew*, for instance, is more like Boswell's *Life of Johnson* than Plato's *Republic*. It has all the reality of living conversation, zig-zagging unpredictably from subject to subject and leading to unexpected triumphs and defeats for the two protagonists. Rameau and the philosopher speak in quite different voices, Rameau's part being full of the colloquial language of the Paris streets and cafés. The dialogue can be read aloud with great pleasure, and on more than one occasion it has been successfully acted on the stage.

Dialogue is not confined to works which can technically be described as such. In many of Diderot's discursive writings the reader is made aware of the existence of other people, people to be argued with, listened to, convinced. They may be present in the text in the form of literal quotation, or their voices may be impersonated, or again they may be challenged or invoked by the writer. The *Refutation of Helvétius* takes, as one might expect, the form of comments on passages quoted from Helvétius's book *On Man* (*De l'Homme*, 1771), but then Diderot takes the dialogue one stage further, imagining the objections that his opponent might make to his own criticisms. The *Salons* are presented as letters to Grimm, editor of the *Correspondance littéraire*, who is addressed personally from time to time and who did in fact, when he included the *Salons* in his newsletter, take the opportunity of mingling his own voice with that of his friend – dialogue in the full sense of the word.

The fiction too, is permeated with dialogue. Almost always in Diderot's stories and novels one is conscious of the narration – who is talking, to whom, where, when, why. Take

Jacques the Fatalist, the most developed example, a novel
which is entirely constructed out of conversations. The basic
dialogue is that between author and reader since, as Diderot
says at the beginning of his short story called *This is not a
Story* (*Ceci n'est pas un conte*, 1772), 'When you tell a story, it
is to someone who listens, and if the story lasts any time it is
unusual for the story-teller not to be interrupted more than
once by the listener' (R 821). In *Jacques*, Diderot puts words
into this reader's mouth, forestalling possible criticisms and
making the reader press him to give information or to tell
stories apparently against his will. (Of course the real readers
– ourselves – are by no means identical with Diderot's imaginary stooge, and he, the real author, is well aware of this.)
The author–reader dialogue generates a narrative which also
centres on a conversation, this time between the valet Jacques
and his master, who likewise tell one another stories, interrupting one another and being in their turn interrupted by the
author or by other story-telling characters. No objective
source of discourse is left intact, but the novel is alive
with echoes of the spoken words with which people fill their
lives.

A tricky question arises at this point: is the frequency of
dialogue in a writer an indication of what might be called a
'dialogic' cast of mind, which is genuinely open to conflicting
points of view? It might at first sight seem obvious that this
is so, and indeed many commentators have made this equation
for Diderot. A contrary case could be made. The dialogue
might be seen as a way of enveloping any potential adversaries, anticipating their possible objections – and this indeed is
how the form is often used for persuasive purposes, for
instance in the philosopher Berkeley's *Dialogues of Hylas and
Philonous*. Such it seems to me is the dialogue in the *Paradox
of the Actor*, or, more interestingly, in the *Conversation of a*

Philosopher with the Maréchale de ***, in which we see a wily Diderot dealing with all the objections raised against atheism by a charming but rather naïve society lady. Compared with such works, the single-minded declaration of personal opinion that one finds for instance in Rousseau's *Émile* might seem more honestly 'dialogic' in that it invites answers without trying to incorporate within itself the adversary's point of view.

In favour of this argument it could also be pointed out that for all the multiplicity of speakers in Diderot's writing, the *voice* that we hear in his writing does not always vary as much as one might expect. This is not true of *Rameau's Nephew*, for there we hear very distinctly the voice of the other. Elsewhere too there are basic distinctions in the manner of speaking between male and female, rich and poor, expert and layman, believer and unbeliever. But equally often (for instance in *D'Alembert's Dream*) there is a merging of voices, so that it is hard, unless one is keeping a close watch on the stage directions, to know quite who is talking. Interestingly enough, this is perhaps most obviously the case with the two plays written in the 1750s, plays which fail in part because of the sameness of the eloquence which runs through all the speeches.

Nevertheless, I do not think it will do to say, as one critic has done, that what we hear in Diderot's writing is essentially an imperious monologue. This would be to overestimate the degree of certainty that he brought to most problems, to overlook the amount of self-criticism and self-mockery that is present in almost all his writings, dialogue or not. True, he will often be carried away by some great theme that is close to his heart, but then he will hesitate, withdraw, see objections or imagine himself into the feelings of those who occupy a quite different position from his own. There are limits to this empathy (Diderot is no Shakespeare), but one only has to read

25

The Nun or *Rameau's Nephew* to see his ability to project himself into another skin.

It also sometimes seems that he enjoys pursuing a paradoxical line of thought as far as it will go; the paradox is the surprising and apparently false assertion which can push the mind to new discoveries. Diderot had learnt the value of such devil's advocacy in his rhetoric training at school, where he is reputed to have been asked to compose a speech for the serpent to make to Eve, and we may do well to bear this in mind when listening to Rameau, of whom he says:

> They [eccentrics like Rameau] disrupt the tedious uniformity which our education, our social conventions and our polite manners have introduced among us. If one of them appears in company, he is like a piece of yeast which ferments and restores to everyone a portion of his natural liberty. He shakes and stirs things up; he calls forth praise and blame; he brings out the truth. (R 425)

For Diderot the truth was not obvious: it had to be 'brought out', and all sorts of tactics were useful for this. It seems probable that the dialogue, together with other strategies of writing, enabled him to fly kites, to test out ideas, preserving a certain distance even from those which were dear to him. Needless to say, this is not at all the same thing as the gift of the dramatist.

We have noted the paradox that Diderot produces a more living dialogue in some non-dramatic works than in the plays which were performed in the public theatre. In part this is the difference between public and private writing. In such works as the *Encyclopedia*, the two plays of the 1750s and the pieces contributed to Raynal's *History of the Two Indies*, Diderot is writing for a broad contemporary public, aiming for an immediate effect in the manner of a preacher, and resorting to a relatively traditional and often emotive eloquence. This

public voice, which goes with the public image of the benefi-
cent philosopher and the man of feeling, is by no means
confined to the more public writings; in those most private
utterances, the letters to Sophie Volland, Diderot sometimes
writes in this way:

My dear, let us live in such a way that our life may be free of
falsehood. The more highly I regard you, the dearer you will be to
me. The more virtuously I behave, the more you will love me. How I
should shun vice, even if I had no other judge than my Sophie!
(C II 145)

This may be embarrassing to a twentieth-century sensibility,
like much of the eloquence of the so-called age of reason, but
modern readers must reaccustom themselves to it if they are to
respond fully to Diderot. However, in the more private
works, such as those first aired in the *Correspondance
littéraire*, this kind of full-blown eloquence alternates with
quite different styles. It is as if the writer was talking in a large
room, but then dropping his voice to say a few words to
intimate friends such as Sophie and Grimm, or to the posterity which meant so much to him. It would be wrong, I think,
to concentrate on the private voice, with all its appealing
irony, and to neglect the louder tones of the public speaker.
Both have their place in Diderot's world.

More generally, indeed, the reader must be on his or her
guard against the temptation to *reduce* Diderot. This is true of
all writers, even of those, such as Rousseau, who like to think
of themselves as offering a unified and coherent message. It is
doubly true for a writer like Diderot, who seems to challenge
the thinking reader to resolve some of the contradictions he
sets before us. Such a caveat applies to attempts at a global
understanding of his thought, but also to the interpretation of
individual books. *Rameau's Nephew* and *Jacques the Fatalist*
in particular have given rise to some very divergent readings.

There is an optimistic tendency among university-based readers to assume that research will enable us to overcome such diversity, showing a given reading to be clearly acceptable or unacceptable. I think this is an illusion – though no doubt a fruitful one – and I believe that as readers we should resist the attempts of critics to close doors. To take one case, *Jacques the Fatalist* is obviously concerned, though how seriously we cannot tell, with the issue implied by its title, the question of freedom and determinism; a second focus is, clearly, problems of verisimilitude, convention and truth. But neither of these is enough in itself to account for the work; other centres of interest appear and disappear as the work progresses: moral questions, comic moments, social considerations and much else. All of these have their place, and I cannot see any justification for the dogmatic assertion that (for instance) Diderot's intentions in writing his novel had nothing to do with social criticism. Naturally all independent-minded readers (and these are Diderot's best readers) will deal freely with him, choosing what they want for their own needs, but they will miss a great deal if they do not lay themselves open to the complexity and many-sidedness of his work. The quest for unity can be a blind alley.

This chapter has been an introduction to Diderot the *writer*, rather than Diderot the philosopher. In the rest of this book greater emphasis will be placed on what could crudely be called the content of his work, the central ideas and questions which impelled him to write. But I hope readers will bear in mind throughout that Diderot is no less interesting as a man who wrote in a certain way than as a man who had certain ideas. Form *is* content, and a good reading of Diderot should not let the two come apart.

4 The free thinker

'The first step towards philosophy is incredulity.' According to Diderot's daughter, these were the last words she heard him speak, the night before he died. They echo what he had written in his first original work, the *Philosophical Thoughts* of 1746: 'Scepticism is the first step towards the truth' (PH 28). Scepticism and incredulity are not exactly the same thing, but the similarity of the two remarks at a distance of nearly forty years points to one central continuity in Diderot's thinking: the urge to call authority in question.

Critical thinking was an essential element in what we call the Enlightenment. Indeed the *philosophes* were seen by their enemies as destroyers, and this view survived and flourished in the nineteenth century, to be enshrined in the famous definition of enlightenment which still figures in the *Shorter Oxford Dictionary*: 'shallow and pretentious intellectualism, unreasonable contempt for authority and tradition, etc.; applied *esp.* to the spirit and aims of the French philosophers of the 18th c.'

The movement goes back well beyond the beginning of the eighteenth century. Two of the great masters of the Enlightenment, Bacon and Descartes, had set the example of rejection of the different idols that governed people's thinking, such idols as the unquestioned authority of great books, great men, custom and superstition. For them, as for such early French Enlighteners as Bayle and Fontenelle – and, in the following generation, Voltaire and Montesquieu – the serious thinker was one who took no authority on trust. An object lesson in incredulity was given by Fontenelle in his *History of the Oracles* (*Histoire des oracles*, 1687): a child was born with a golden tooth in Silesia, the fame of the tooth spread far and wide, learned men gave their opinions, and only then was it discovered that the whole thing was a fraud, a layer of gold foil applied to a perfectly ordinary tooth. This little tale could have many applications, and the lesson was not lost on the Diderot who wrote in his *Philosophical Thoughts*: 'Even if the whole of Paris told me that a dead man had been resurrected at Passy, I would not believe a word of it' (PH 37). He himself was not exempt from credulity and was ready to believe for instance in the dubious experiments by the scientists Buffon and Needham which 'demonstrated' the possibility of the spontaneous generation of living beings from dead matter; but a great deal of his thinking started from suspicion, and he seems to have derived positive pleasure from undermining, exposing and demystifying. In this chapter I shall follow the working of this critical impulse in three main areas: religion, sexuality and politics.

Incredulity suggests above all religious disbelief. The Catholic Church occupied a commanding position in Diderot's France; even though we can see the beginnings of dechristianisation in certain aspects of eighteenth-century social life, the clergy were still the first order of the kingdom, churches and religious orders were everywhere and the orthodox faith was given the backing of the secular power. In particular the Church largely controlled the educational system and had an important say in the control of publication. For a questioning *philosophe* who wanted to liberate thought from its traditional chains, the Church represented a threat and an obstacle, however liberal individual members of the clergy might be in their beliefs and habits.

We have seen that Diderot came from a solidly religious background. His brother was a priest, he himself received the tonsure, studied theology and might well have taken orders (it appears that he went through a religious phase at school and wanted to become a Jesuit). Although the Catholic authorities were in part responsible for some of his troubles, hostility to the Church was never to be as dominant a theme in his writing as in Voltaire's, but intermittently throughout his life he felt the need to challenge the religion of his upbringing. It is not clear that he managed to cut himself completely adrift from it, however confident his atheism might appear; certainly his fiction and his art criticism show a continuing ability to identify with Christian attitudes.

In his early philosophical writings we can see a fairly rapid move away from orthodox faith. The *Philosophical Thoughts* were reputedly written over the Easter weekend of 1746; their title is an answer to Pascal's famous *Pensées*, an apologia for Christianity. Towards the end of the book, Diderot declares: 'I was born in the catholic and apostolic Church of Rome and I submit with all my power to its decisions; I wish to die in the religion of my fathers' (PH 46). The work as a whole produces a different impression. It is made up of loosely linked fragments and incorporates several voices, in particular the deist, the atheist and the sceptic. Christianity is attacked from the outset, mainly for its denial of human feelings. Soon an atheist makes his appearance, a classic atheist who owes a good deal to Spinoza and Bayle as well as to the ancient philosophers. His first argument is one that will recur more than once in Diderot's writing: 'Just because I cannot conceive how movement, which is so well able to maintain the universe, was able to give birth to it, it is ridiculous to meet this difficulty by supposing the existence of a being whom I am equally unable to conceive (PH 15–16).' Notions of creation and of a spiritual being only lead to another enigma; the atheist has as yet no explanation of his own (or at any rate not one that Diderot can

31

endorse), but he rejects an explanation which only rephrases the problem in other terms.

The second argument is the familiar argument known as Bayle's paradox, and this too reappears in Diderot's later writing: 'If everything is the work of a God, everything must be as good as it could possibly be; for if everything is not as good as it could possibly be, this must indicate in God a lack of power or a lack of good will' (PH 16). The problem of evil is one which taxed many eighteenth-century thinkers; it is an objection not to the existence of a God, but to the existence of a God who is good in human terms.

The atheist does not have it all his own way at this stage. Diderot has no time for a religion that depends on revelation, but he still seems to have faith in the deist's rational argument from design – that the order of the universe, particularly as revealed in the new science of the time, proves the existence of an intelligent creator. It is a familiar argument, and is expounded here fairly briefly, but it apparently satisfied Diderot in 1746 – and he still felt it necessary to attribute to atheism harmful moral effects.

More important, however, is the stress on scepticism in this early work. Scepticism does not here mean a total unwillingness to believe in anything; this is what Diderot calls 'Pyrrhonism', and he remarks that 'incredulity is sometimes the failing of a fool' (PH 28). A sceptic on the other hand is 'a philosopher who has doubted everything he believes and who believes what a legitimate use of his reason and his senses has shown him to be true' (PH 27-8). This is a moderate form of scepticism, comparable to Descartes's methodical doubt, a necessary preliminary in the search for truth.

Later in his career, Diderot returned to the question of scepticism, notably in the first dialogue of *D'Alembert's Dream*, where he presents his colleague as one who abstains from forming opinions when he cannot be sure. Diderot himself, who is d'Alembert's interlocutor in this dialogue, challenges this notion, suggesting that we cannot remain in a position of indecision; although we may hesitate and waver, we can and must hold beliefs: 'In all things our real opinion is not the one in which we have never wavered, but the one to which we have most frequently returned' (PH 283). I shall discuss the search for constant principles in the next chapter; let us note for the moment that scepticism was a necessary element in Diderot's philosophical enterprise, and that it remained an ever-present alternative for him.

His second philosophical work, which is rather unsatisfactory in conception and execution and was not to be published until 1830, does in fact have the word 'sceptic' in the title. *The Sceptic's Walk* contains another inconclusive debate about religion and metaphysics, with deists, sceptics and a persuasive devotee of the pantheist philosophy of Spinoza. However, it was with the *Letter on the Blind* of 1749 (the work which earned him imprisonment at Vincennes) that Diderot's questioning of orthodox religion and philosophy became really radical. The *Letter*, written in its author's familiar digressive form, covers several different topics. It begins with what was called Molyneux's problem: would a man born blind, who had learned to distinguish a cube from a sphere by touch, be able to distinguish them visually if his sight was restored to him? What is at issue here is the origin of our ideas and their relation to our sense impressions, questions of great importance to Locke and his philosophical followers, including Diderot's friend Condillac. Diderot, however, rather than discuss the question in the abstract, seeks to involve himself in the actual world of the blind, examining the actions, words and opinions of a number of blind people. In *D'Alembert's Dream* he will use real but strange exceptions to the norm as a help to new thoughts; similarly in this *Letter* he uses the blind man, a 'monster' in the world of the seeing, in order to question some unquestioned beliefs.

One example of this critical approach comes towards the beginning of the work, where Diderot, after discussing a blind man's understanding of mirrors, remarks that such examples should make us cautious about assuming that what goes on in other people's minds is analogous to what goes on in our own. This may seem inoffensive, but such arguments take on a more polemic edge when the existence and nature of God are at stake. Putting words into the mouth of a blind Cambridge mathematician, Saunderson, Diderot now casts doubt on the rational deism of the *Philosophical Thoughts*. On his deathbed, the blind man objects to a Protestant minister that the argument from design is weak to one who cannot see. The very existence of blind people and similar 'monsters' casts doubt upon the sublime order of the deists, and in any case, even if there is an order which satisfies us, there is no necessary connection between this and a 'sovereignly intelligent being'. Diderot again points to the folly of providing an incomprehensible answer (God) to an insoluble puzzle (the universe). But now he goes one stage further, sketching a vision of a natural world in a state of constant flux, in which our present 'order', the order which justified the argument from design, is just a passing moment:

What is this world, Mr Holmes? A compound which is subject to changes, all of them indicating a continual tendency towards destruction; a rapid succession of beings which follow one another, push one another on, and disappear; a passing symmetry; a momentary order. (PH 123)

For the time being this is no more than a flash of vision on Diderot's part. Later he will attempt to evolve a more systematic account of the universe of matter in movement, and I shall say something about this in the next chapter. In any case, the *Letter on the Blind* seems to represent its author's crucial break not only with Christianity, but with the relatively reassuring deism which replaced the traditional faith for many eighteenth-century thinkers, from Voltaire to Benjamin Franklin. I say 'seems', because one can rarely be entirely sure of Diderot's position on any subject. In this work, for instance, shortly after his vision of meaningless flux, the dying Saunderson utters his last cry: 'Oh God of Clarke and Newton, have pity on me!' – suggesting that the God of reason retains his appeal for the incredulous philosopher. It is important to remember the difficulty for a person of Diderot's generation of living entirely outside the comforting framework which various forms of religion provided for most of his contemporaries.

Whatever his personal needs, he often returns in his later work to the critique of religion, above all Christianity. The influence of his brother is a matter for speculation, but I should guess that the two men pushed one another in opposite directions. Certainly Canon Diderot came to typify for the *philosophe* an inhumane and intolerant faith which is attacked and mocked in many of his works, from the *Encyclopedia* to such unofficial pieces as the *Conversation of a Philosopher with the Maréchale de* ***.

The *Encyclopedia* was a public work, and one would not expect it to contain all-out attacks on the official religion of the country. Diderot was careful to include a certain amount of orthodox theology, but he also found more or less indirect ways of discrediting the doctrines and practices of the Church. Thus a famous cross-reference at the end of a respectful article on the Franciscans ('Cordeliers') sends the reader to the article 'Capuchon', which tells unedifying tales of the petty squabbles about dress which divided the order. There

35

are also articles which drive home the lessons of Bayle or Fontenelle on the scrutiny of evidence, and numerous accounts of the philosophy and religion of other peoples allow for all kinds of suggestive parallels to be drawn. But if the *Encyclopedia* is to be considered an anti-religious work (as undoubtedly it was at the time), this is due above all to the this-worldly bias of a publication in which the manufacture of useful objects bulks larger than the problems of theology.

In less public writings, Diderot attacks Christianity more openly, playing his part in a campaign which had been gathering momentum throughout the century. An 'Addition' to the *Philosophical Thoughts*, published in 1762 and largely based on an anonymous anti-Christian tract, is much fiercer than the work of 1746. Christianity – like other revealed religions – is not only a scandal to reason, but a source of misery. The concluding fragment imagines a misanthropist out to avenge himself on the human race:

What can I do to punish them for their unjust actions and to make them as miserable as they deserve? Ah, if only I could find a way of setting their minds on some great imaginary being which they would regard as more important than their own lives and about which they could never agree. (PH 72)

The answer of course is 'God', the source of endless questioning, dispute, hate and bloodshed.

A similar critique of what the radical *philosophes* called superstition or fanaticism is to be found in Diderot's contributions to the *History of the Two Indies*, and more elegantly and succinctly in the little *Conversation of a Philosopher with the Maréchale of* ***. In the latter work his main and almost his only concern is the moral consequences of belief. He is at pains to show that there is no connection between religion and morality, that it is perfectly possible and reasonable to be a good man and an atheist. And again he carries the attack into the enemy camp, suddenly interrupting an urbane conversation with a diatribe against the intolerance which he sees as inseparable from religious faith: 'Christ said that he had come to separate the husband from the wife, the mother from the children, the friend from the friend, and his prophecy has been only too faithfully fulfilled' (PH 533).

Diderot is happy in this dialogue to accept the label of unbeliever, declaring himself unmoved by the threats and promises of Christianity. It is certainly the case that in his later writings, whatever residual sympathy he may have felt for religious attitudes, he calmly allied himself with such atheists as his friend d'Holbach against what he called the 'great prejudice'. Unlike d'Holbach, however, and unlike Voltaire in his campaign against the *infâme* (the Roman Catholic Church), Diderot does not seem to have pursued the religion of his fathers with great venom. In 1768 he noted with amusement in a letter to Sophie that 'it is raining cannon-balls in the house of the Lord' (C VIII 234), but his own concerns go far beyond this negative anti-Christianity. This can be seen in his novel *The Nun*.

The Nun grew out of a hoax. To lure a friend, the marquis de Croismare, back to Paris, Diderot, Grimm and one or two others had sent him appeals for help which purported to come from Suzanne Simonin, a refugee from a convent. The fake letters convinced the marquis, but the joke backfired on Diderot, who became so absorbed in the nun that he made her the heroine of a fictitious memoir of considerable proportions. We follow her lamentable path through convent life, and it is a black picture, not far removed from a Gothic horror novel. There are scenes of depravity and torture, described with a breathless intensity characteristic of Diderot in moments of excitement. The effect of accumulation is such that the narrator has to forestall the objection of readers: ' "Such numerous, diverse and uninterrupted horrors! Such a sequence of elaborate tortures from religious believers! It is not true to life'', they will say.' She replies blandly that her story is strange but true; what providence has done (Diderot rather than providence, we may comment) is to pour down on one head 'a mass of cruel deeds which are distributed, according to its impenetrable decrees, over an infinite multitude of unfortunate beings who had come before her in the convent and who would follow her' (R 307). All of this might seem to serve a familiar Enlightenment critique of monastic life – and indeed convents are openly attacked by Suzanne's lawyer, Manoury, at a crucial point in the book. Even so, the interest of *The Nun* does not lie principally in the denunciation of forced vows, convents or Catholicism. The novel was not published in book form in Diderot's lifetime, so it seems improbable that he meant it as a campaigning work. What strikes the reader rather, as so often in Diderot, is his urge to lift the veil, to penetrate to hidden places, to tell secrets. His attitude to nuns is like his attitude to the blind: they can tell him something new about humanity. Thinking about monasteries and convents, he asks: What happens to normal human beings in such (to him) unnatural surroundings? The novel is like the account of a scientific experiment; Diderot's questioning is one of curiosity rather than negative criticism.

Of course the experiment is a fiction; in the picture of the cloistered life it is not easy to tell how much comes from personal (if second-hand) knowledge, how much from deduction or imagination. Thus one aspect of his exposure which has caught the interest of many readers is the vivid depiction of a lesbian Mother Superior. This is done from the point of view of the naïve Suzanne, with appropriate tones of shock ('What a woman, monsieur le marquis, what an abominable woman!'), and it seems probable that Diderot shared his heroine's rejection of female homosexuality, which is seen as the 'natural' result of an 'unnatural' situation. At the same time, his treatment of the Mother Superior betrays a fascination for this taboo subject – a subject which worried him personally because of his agonised suspicions about the relations between Sophie Volland and her younger sister. These are secrets he wants to know more about.

As far as we know, Diderot's own sex life was fairly conventional for the easy-going milieu in which he lived, but in discussing sexual matters he habitually shows the same unorthodox spirit which we have seen in his treatment of religion. Enemies of the *philosophes* linked free thinking and loose living; the word 'libertin', originally meaning a free thinker, came to have the meaning now associated with the English 'libertine'. And whatever can be said about the actual behaviour of the *philosophes* (many of them very respectable citizens), their writings quite often season critical philosophising with sexual discussions which are deliberately scurrilous (one thinks of Voltaire's gleeful exploitation of the more shocking passages from the Old Testament).

One of Diderot's earliest works, *The Indiscreet Jewels*, is just such a blend of serious intellectual concerns with merry pornography, and a similar mixture is to be found in several of his later works, particularly the more private ones. In *D'Alembert's Dream*, for instance, the discussion of difficult biological questions is interrupted by a not unrelated erotic dream, and the exploration of materialism is extended into some wanton speculation on the morality of cross-breeding. Diderot is well aware that what he writes will scandalise some readers. His rhetorical strategy in the dialogue is to have the doctor Bordeu expound his adventurous opinions to a female interlocutor who is by turns shocked and unshockable. Bordeu says:

I do not let myself be fooled by words, and I express my ideas all the more freely because my spotless reputation makes me secure against all attacks. I ask you then, of two acts, both of which involve only pleasure and can merely be pleasurable, not useful, but one of which gives pleasure only to the agent whereas the other allows the pleasure to be shared with another being, male or female . . . which one will be favoured by common sense? (PH 379)

Reading such passages, and others like them in the letters to Sophie Volland and elsewhere, one senses the enjoyable explosion of freedom in a mind which can wander far from the tracks of orthodoxy.

Light-hearted such discussions may be at times, but they belong to a quite serious questioning of the sexual mores of French society. We have seen that in *D'Alembert's Dream* Bordeu wants to distinguish between his pure behaviour and his free thoughts ('I would not raise my hat in the street to a man who was suspected of putting my teaching into practice'). There is a disquieting but necessary gap between theory and practice here. Diderot too appears as a guardian of orthodox morality in some of his dealings, but in his writings he feels free to undermine the values which his society officially imposed on him, like it or not. *The Indiscreet Jewels* can be read at one level as a protest against the hypocrisy of society in sexual matters, or even a plea for the rights of the body. Subsequently Diderot comes back repeatedly to the various rules and prohibitions governing relations between the sexes, submitting them to the same sort of radical scrutiny which he gives to religious belief and practice. In an episode in his correspondence with Sophie Volland he poses a *cas de conscience*: a woman wants to have a child, but does not want to be married; she asks a man to father the child without any further commitment on either side – is she right or wrong and can he reasonably agree to her proposal? (Diderot is careful to reassure Sophie that he is not the man in question.)

Oaths of faithfulness are a particular target for his satire, whether he is telling the humorous story of the knife and the sheath in *Jacques the Fatalist* (see p. 106), or indulging in this kind of philosophical meditation:

The first vows sworn by two creatures of flesh and blood were made at the foot of a rock that was crumbling to dust; they called as witness to their constancy a heaven which never stays the same for one moment; everything within them and around them was changing, and they thought their hearts were exempt from vicissitudes. Children! (R 632)

Looked at from this perspective, marriage vows appear as foolish as the monastic vows whose results we see in *The Nun*.

Diderot draws our attention then to 'the disadvantage of attaching moral ideas to certain physical actions which do not require them' – to quote the subtitle of his most sustained critique of European sexual mores, the *Supplement to Bougainville's Voyage*. This 'supplement' is inspired by the idyllic chapters on Tahiti in Bougainville's account of his travels. The 'myth of Tahiti', as one of Diderot's interlocutors calls it, had a considerable effect on European readers, providing a stimulating new variant on the theme of the noble savage. In the central section of the *Supplement*, a conversation between an islander and a French ship's chaplain, Tahiti provides Diderot with a foil against which European practices can be made to stand out as indefensibly absurd:

OROU. Does the woman who has sworn to belong only to her husband never give herself to another man?

CHAPLAIN. Nothing is more common.

OROU. Your lawgivers either punish her or not: if they punish her, they are ferocious animals attacking nature; if not, they are weaklings who have held their authority up to scorn by a useless prohibition.

CHAPLAIN: The guilty women who escape the severity of the laws are punished by general disapproval.

OROU: In other words justice is exercised by the lack of common sense of the entire nation, and the folly of public opinion comes to the aid of the laws. (PH 482-3)

And so on. This section comes after a similar assault on the Chaplain's religion, very much in the style of Voltaire. In both, Diderot uses a familiar eighteenth-century technique which one might call the 'innocent eye' to highlight the strangeness of 'normal' customs.

Of course it was easy for Diderot to write like this. His idyllic fantasies did not solve the real problems that faced him. The dialogue between Orou and the Chaplain is followed by a dialogue between two French men of the world which makes it clear that it is easier to undermine than to construct. Diderot's imaginative exploration of the subject could perhaps be called irresponsible; it does not commit him to any particular line, nor (since the *Supplement* is yet another work which was not printed till well after his death) is he intent on reforming the actual state of society. Rather than preach, he is doing what he describes in the opening lines of *Rameau's Nephew*, where he says that he pursues ideas as young men pursued loose women in the Palais Royal gardens. The comparison is a significant one – as is the image of lifting nature's veil, which is prominent in the *Thoughts on the Interpretation of Nature*. Philosophy must be immodest.

Whether or not we call it irresponsible, Diderot's irreverent attitude to the foundations of existing society certainly prefigures the critical or negative stance which we nowadays associate with the intellectual. 'Beware of those who impose order', says one of the speakers in the *Supplement*. Diderot is naturally suspicious of established authority. He himself, though he knew many of the rich and powerful, never occupied any official position in France, and in the one case where he approached the position of court favourite, with Catherine of Russia, his familiar critical attitude quickly became apparent.

For of course politics is the other major area in which his subversive urge could come into play. In *The Sceptic's Walk*, one of the main interlocutors, Ariste, seems to be speaking for the author when he declares: 'Make me keep quiet about religion and politics, and I have nothing more to say' (O II 81). Not that Diderot can be reckoned a major figure in the history of political thought. It is rather that here too we see his questioning instinct asserting itself and leading him to a radical position.

From the beginning he cast doubt on political absolutism. His first political writing, the *Encyclopedia* article 'Political Authority', can be seen as undermining the theories which buttressed the idea of absolute monarchy. It begins with these words: 'No man has received from nature the right to command other men. Freedom is a present from heaven, and every individual of the same species has the right to enjoy it as soon as he enjoys reason' (P 9). One may question this conception of rights and point to a confusion here between a hypothetical state of nature and the actual state of people living in society, but there is no doubt that these opening sentences ring out with a challenging vigour. It is like the eloquence of Diderot's friend Rousseau, though the theory of the *Social Contract* is different from that expounded in this article. What matters for both men is to safeguard the freedom of individual people against the apparently rational claims of various kinds of authority. To Diderot's hostile critics, the principles of his article were 'contrary to the supreme authority, to the constitution of the French Empire and to public peace'.

It would be wrong to present the editor of the *Encyclopedia* as a seditious writer. He was a patriot and he wanted his country to conform more closely to the ideal model of a constitutional monarchy, but little of his writing could be called revolutionary. In the *Philosophical Thoughts*, admittedly with a view to attacking Christianity, he declares that 'any innovation is to be feared in a government' (PH 32). The royal power had him imprisoned, the Parlement outlawed the *Encyclopedia*, but he always refused the possibility of going abroad to continue his work in freer conditions.

Perhaps his attitude to political authority, as to authority in general, is best defined as one of *mistrust*. This is particularly obvious in his last decade or so, when he confronted the so-called enlightened despots of his age. Some at least of the *philosophes* saw the main hope for rational reform in the conversion of powerful monarchs to enlightened principles, and were willing to throw in their lot with Frederick of Prussia or Catherine of Russia. Diderot never had much time for Frederick; in 1770 and 1774 he wrote some fierce denunciations of the philosopher-king, in whom he saw a Machiavellian tyrant. Catherine on the contrary was his protector. In some of his letters he praises her as a wonderful combination of Cleopatra and Caesar. He was certainly flattered by her favour and felt that as her philosopher he was doing something for the cause of political reform. But he did not give up his independence and in due course aroused her indignation by the critical comments he wrote on the *Nakaz*, the 'instruction' which she had drawn up for the assembly which was to draft a constitution for Russia. She discovered these comments after his death and dismissed them, saying: 'If my Instruction had been to Diderot's liking, it would have been calculated to turn everything upside down.' Diderot was an irresponsible child, a disruptive force.

The *Observations on the Nakaz* are in fact based on the same democratic principle as the article on 'Political Authority'. By now the expression is more forthright; the prologue begins with the words: 'There is no true sovereign other than the nation. There can be no true legislator other than the people.' What Diderot is defending is the right of a people to control its own destiny. What makes him suspicious is the authority that claims to know best what is good for its subordinates. However enlightened Catherine may be, she is in fact a despot, and he challenges her to abdicate her despotic power and submit herself to the authority of her people and their laws:

If on reading what I have written and listening to her conscience, her heart quivers with joy, then she no longer wants to rule over slaves; if she trembles, if her blood runs cold, if she goes pale, then she has thought herself better than she is. (P 345)

The particular danger of the enlightened despot is that he or she lulls the people into a trustful negligence. Against Frederick the Great's maxim that 'nothing is better than the arbitrary government of just, humane and virtuous princes', Diderot asserts that 'the arbitrary government of a just and enlightened prince is always bad. His virtues are the most dangerous and effective of all seductions.' Without the right of opposition – even when it is misused – 'subjects resemble a flock of sheep whose cries are ignored on the pretext that they are being led to lush pastures' (PH 620). The same fear is voiced in one of his last writings, an eloquent harangue to the American revolutionaries, warning them against the danger of great leaders. He anticipates the slogan that the price of freedom is eternal vigilance.

At the limit, this questioning vigilance can involve the right to violent insurrection. Diderot was not a revolutionary, but in those of his later works which remained anonymous or unpublished, he sometimes makes statements that prefigure the trial and execution of Louis XVI. The opening section of the *Observations on the Nakaz* states that the first article of a proper constitution should include a declaration by the sovereign that 'if we should change or break the law . . . it is right that the people should be released from the oath of fidelity, that it should prosecute us, depose us and even, if necessary, condemn us to death' (P 343–4). This is an exceptionally audacious moment for Diderot, and must be set against the far more moderate tone which is common in his writing about France. Nevertheless it does seem that as he got older, far from growing more conservative, he became increasingly susceptible to the appeal of a kind of rebellious heroism. Many of his contributions to Raynal's *History of the Two Indies* consist of diatribes against the abuses of colonial power, and on occasion, as in this passage against British East India Company, his eloquence becomes vehement:

No, no, sooner or later justice must be done. If this were not to happen, I should speak to the population in these terms: 'Peoples, whose roar has so often made your masters tremble, what are you waiting for? For what occasion are you keeping your torches and the stones that pave your streets? Tear them up . . .' (PD 311)

These lines were quoted with horror as a harbinger of revolution by the Bonapartist marquis de La Rochefoucauld-Liancourt in 1809. The prudent Diderot did not assume responsibility for them, but in 1781, in one of his last writings, he defended Raynal's courage in signing a work for which he had been driven into exile: 'The people says: "Life first, then philosophy". But the man who has assumed the mantle of Socrates, and who loves truth and virtue more than his life will say: "Philosophy first, then life" '(PH 629).

In defending Raynal, Diderot knew that he himself was not going to sacrifice his life for truth, but all his life he saw Socrates as an ideal. In prison in Vincennes, he spent his time translating Plato's *Apology* into French, in his *Discourse on Dramatic Poetry* he envisaged a heroic drama of the death of Socrates, and his friends sometimes called him 'brother Plato'. In *Rameau's Nephew*, 'Myself' defends Socrates against the cynical attacks of Rameau, who claims that the Greek philosopher was an 'audacious and bizarre individual', a 'turbulent' citizen who encouraged foolish people to break good laws by his contempt for bad ones (R 429–30).

Whether the virtuous citizen could place himself above the law was a problem that Diderot never resolved. As we have seen, a great deal of his writing tends logically to non-acceptance, yet his sense of the importance of social bonds made him hesitate before recommending positive disobedience. His more common position is the 'enlightened' one recommended by one of the speakers in the *Supplement to Bougainville's Voyage*: 'We shall speak against the senseless laws until they are reformed, and in the meantime we shall obey them' (PH 515). But while one may distinguish between words and deeds, there is no getting away from the fact that words as well as deeds can undermine the established order. Socrates was the individual who called in question the accepted values and beliefs of his society. As a subversive he was treated as a public enemy, and as such he is Diderot's hero:

It may happen that this being falls victim to prejudice and the laws; but there are two sorts of law, those of absolute equity and universality, and the bizarre ones which owe their authority only to blindness or to the force of circumstance. The latter merely cover the

47

man who is guilty of breaking them with a passing disgrace, which time then transfers to the judges and the nations, on whom it remains for ever. (R 401)

For the destroyer is also a creator. This chapter has been concerned with the hostility to authority which informs Diderot's thinking in various fields. He encourages his reader to mistrust orthodoxies of all kinds; he appeals to our critical spirit and our love of freedom. The more positive side of this is that for him thinking is an adventure. The loss of old certainties is not a cause for regret, but of hope for the future. No longer trusting in the traditional order, we can search for a new one. There is a sense of great excitement at the vistas that open up to the unbeliever in a great deal of what can be called Diderot's philosophical writing, in the *Letter on the Blind*, the *Thoughts on the Interpretation of Nature*, or *D'Alembert's Dream*.

It is true that there is an underlying scepticism which surfaces even in some of his most positive writing. In the *Thoughts on the Interpretation of Nature*, for instance, among discussions of scientific method, we read the following:

If all beings are in a state of perpetual change, if nature is still at work, then in spite of the chain which binds all phenomena together, there can be no philosophy. All of our natural science becomes as ephemeral as the words we use. What we take for the history of nature is only the very incomplete history of one moment. (PH 240–1)

The doubting impulse is still there – and I shall return to it in Chapter 6, but in spite of this the overriding mood of the book is one of confidence. Although the world of knowledge is a great dark space with scattered points of light, it may be possible to extend these and create new ones. Diderot speaks enthusiastically of the inspired guessing of the scientist; even the wildest conjectures can lead to discoveries. And the philosopher must have faith that eventually all these discoveries will be brought together in a new order – the order of nature.

5 The order of nature

The history of thought in eighteenth-century France is often presented in terms of a conflict between rationalism and empiricism. On the one hand are those whose aim is to work out reasoned systems of philosophy, great edifices of conceptual thought which explain the totality of things. Opposed to them are the enemies of systems: believing, with Locke, that all our ideas originate in sense impressions (already a sizeable hypothesis), they devote themselves to observable facts, and are suspicious of the great constructions of such philosophers as Descartes, Leibniz or Spinoza – let alone Plato. In reality, of course, few thinkers fit neatly into either camp.

The previous two chapters have stressed the disruptive, questioning element in Diderot's writing, but this is not the whole picture. Perhaps because he was temperamentally inclined to free exploration, more a nightingale than a cuckoo, he also felt very strongly the desire for order. Chaos excited him, alarmed him and made him want to master it. The disruptive, questioning approach which I discussed in the previous chapter is usually the first step towards the discovery or creation of a new, more satisfying order. The history of his thinking can be seen as a series of attempts to formulate rational systems of explanation – of the physical world, of moral, social and political behaviour, of aesthetics. As the next chapter will show, he was too perceptive (and too good a writer) not to admit objections to the orders he proposes, but that does not prevent him from aiming at a global understanding of the natural world and man's place within it.

The belief that everything that exists forms one great,

connected system is one that has inspired philosophers and scientists for centuries. In Diderot's time it took the classic form of the Great Chain of Being, in which all the phenomena of nature could be assigned their rightful place. Such a notion is quite explicitly stated at several points in the work that is sometimes regarded as its author's 'discourse on method', the *Thoughts on the Interpretation of Nature*. For instance, discussing a theory put forward by the philosopher Maupertuis, Diderot asks rhetorically:

I ask him . . . whether the universe or the general collection of all thinking and feeling molecules forms a whole or not. If he replies that it does not form a whole, he will be undermining with a single word the existence of God by introducing disorder into the universe, and he will be destroying the basis of philosophy by breaking the chain that links all beings. (PH 229)

Here the postulate of unity is linked with God; although Diderot will try to explain the universe without recourse to God, in his philosophy he is seeking a substitute for the satisfying universe of his fathers. Nature will replace God.

This prophetic work looks far ahead, to a time when, thanks to a proper combination of deductive reasoning, hypothesis, empirical observation and experiment, the dark places of ignorance will be conquered by the light of scientific knowledge (such is the rhetoric of the Encyclopedist). Diderot is conscious of the limited achievements of the science of his day, but confident that a real beginning has been made on the enterprise which Francis Bacon had advocated 150 years earlier, the advancement of learning. Bacon's influence is visible throughout the *Thoughts on the Interpretation of Nature*, and he was indeed one of the chosen ancestors of the *Encyclopedia*.

Order is of the essence of encyclopedias. In a stock-taking article which is actually entitled 'Encyclopedia', Diderot

51

declares that 'the aim of an encyclopedia is to gather together the knowledge which is scattered over the surface of the earth, and to expose the general system of knowledge to those with whom we live' (O VII 174). The words 'general system' imply an underlying coherence, and it was one of his objectives in the *Encyclopedia* to lay out his material so that these inter-relationships were evident. It was not possible to achieve the God's-eye view of which d'Alembert had spoken in his Preliminary Discourse to the work, a vantage point from which 'the whole universe would be simply a single fact, one great truth.' But one might hope to place the reader on an eminence from which 'it would not be a tortuous labyrinth in which you lose yourself and can see no further than the place where you are standing, but a vast avenue stretching into the distance . . .' (O VII 212). This was to be achieved by a *plan*, laying out the different fields of knowledge – or alternatively the diagram of the tree of knowledge – and by the constant use of cross-references to link one article with all related ones. Likewise Diderot was conscious of the need for order within each article. In particular he set great store by the description of technological processes, which was so important a feature of the work and its greatest claim to usefulness. These descriptions were to be clear and exhaustive, following the same general order and attempting to introduce a more uniform terminology into activities which had grown up in a hap-hazard way. The beautiful plates which make up such a huge part of the complete work also contribute to an attractive image of rational human labour exploiting the natural world in an orderly and productive manner.

Such was the ideal of the *Encyclopedia*. In fact the finished product was considerably more chaotic than all this suggests; it hardly puts the reader in the position of clear-sighted mastery which Diderot envisaged. Nor indeed could the

Encyclopedia, written as it was by many hands (and in many voices), expound a single system of thought. It is true that one can detect in numerous articles a common belief in the primacy of sense experience, together with an insistence on the value of experiment, and there are others which point cryptically towards a new way of thinking, but Diderot was not really able to use this great public compilation as a vehicle for his own theories about the nature of the universe and man's place within it. These are to be found rather in the *Letter on the Blind*, the *Thoughts on the Interpretation of Nature* and, above all, *D'Alembert's Dream*.

The last of these works consists of a sequence of three dialogues, written in the summer of 1769. It is the culmination of a long period of thought in which Diderot tried to work out a completely materialist theory of existence. The deism which we find in the *Philosophical Thoughts* – though by no means unchallenged – proclaims a complex but unchanging world order, designed and sustained by God, a supremely good and rational being. Such an order is compatible with the cosmology of Newton, as it had been with that of Descartes. It usually implies, though this is not spelt out in the *Philosophical Thoughts*, a distinction between two substances, *matter*, which is characterised by the property of 'extension' (i.e. it occupies a given place in space), and *spirit*, which is characterised by thought. In this way God is distinguished from the physical world and the human soul from the human body. It is this distinction, or *dualism*, which provides the initial problem in *D'Alembert's Dream*:

I admit [says Diderot's interlocutor, d'Alembert] that a being which exists somewhere and which does not correspond to any point in space; a being which has no extension, and which occupies extended space and is present beneath every part of this space; which differs in essence from matter and is united to it: which moves it and is moved by it without moving; which acts upon it and is influenced by all its

53

modifications; a being of which I have not the least idea – I admit that such a being is hard to accept. (PH 257)

This challenge to the matter–spirit dualism (and indeed to the idea of God) highlights some of the difficulties encountered by the followers of Descartes. How, for instance, if the mind is immaterial, can one explain the way in which I decide (mentally) to raise my hand, and my muscles contract (physically) in the necessary way for my hand to be raised? Is there, as Descartes suggested, a sort of middle ground, located in a part of the brain called the pineal gland, where the two substances somehow interact? Or is there, as Leibniz argued, a 'pre-established harmony' which makes thought coincide miraculously with action? Such notions seemed absurd to many thinkers of the eighteenth century, but as d'Alembert goes on to point out at the beginning of the dialogue, 'other obscurities await those who reject [them]'. If one was to avoid dualism, it was necessary to eliminate one of the two substances, declaring either that there is nothing but spirit, or that there is nothing but matter. The former position, idealism, is defended by the British philosopher Berkeley, who argued that as thinking beings we can only have knowledge of ideas; if we say that there is a tree in front of us, this means merely that we have formed certain ideas to which we give this name, but we have no way of knowing that there is a material substance in the world that corresponds to these ideas.

Diderot knew Berkeley's idealism, calling it an 'extravagant system . . . which to the shame of the human mind and of philosophy is the most difficult of all to refute, even though it is the most absurd of all systems' (PH 114). He himself, from the time of the *Letter on the Blind*, looked rather to materialism, which corresponded better with his fundamentally non-religious cast of thought, and which offered a more fruitful basis for the scientific study of human life.

Materialism was very much a minority view in eighteenth-century France – indeed it was a scandalous view. It had nevertheless a distinguished ancestry. Diderot himself was influenced not only by contemporaries such as La Mettrie, author of *Man a Machine* (*L'Homme-machine*), but by the ancient Epicurean doctrine expounded for instance in the *De Rerum Natura* of the Latin poet Lucretius. A view of this kind is advanced by the spokesman for atheism in the *Philosophical Thoughts*; assuming that matter is eternal, and that movement is essential to it, as it changes its position over infinite time and space it must, according to the laws of probability, eventually arrange itself in the relatively durable and (to us) satisfactory order which we are tempted to attribute to an act of intelligent creation: 'Thus the mind should be more surprised by the hypothetical duration of chaos than by the actual birth of the universe' (PH 23).

Such a speculative theory of matter in movement allows Diderot to suggest an alternative to the idea of creation. It does not, however, take him very far towards an explanation of how matter is made up and how it behaves. And it tells one very little about the nature and behaviour of living beings – and above all of human beings. It was these questions which increasingly attracted Diderot as he turned his attention from mathematics and physics (still very important in the *Letter on the Blind*) to the rapidly developing sciences of biology, chemistry and medicine. In the two decades after 1750 he studied these subjects enthusiastically if spasmodically, keeping abreast of recent developments, so that by the time he came to write *D'Alembert's Dream* (yet another work of private exploration) he was able to put forward hypotheses for a materialist explanation not only of animal life, but also of human feeling and thought.

His fundamental idea is that all matter possesses 'sensi-

bility', the ability to feel. This may remain latent, but it
is made active when a 'dead' molecule is assimilated to others
which are 'living'. The prime example of this is eating:

When you eat, what do you do? You remove the obstacles which prevented the sensibility of the food from becoming active. You assimi-
late it to yourself, you make flesh of it, you animalise it, you make it
capable of feeling. (PH 261)

Thus he throws a bridge between the animate and the
inanimate. It is a shaky bridge, as he realises ('If I cannot solve
the problem you set me, at least I come very near to doing so').
He finds support for the theory of universal sensibility in the
recent experiments of Needham and Buffon, who had claimed
(mistakenly) to have observed the process of spontaneous generation. Further corroboration came from studies of the development of the embryo; there is an eloquent passage on the egg:

Do you see this egg? It is with this that we can overturn all the schools
of theology and all the temples on earth. What is the egg? An insensible
mass until the germ is introduced into it. And what is it after the germ
has been introduced? Still an insensible mass, for the germ itself is only
a crude and inert fluid. And how will this mass acquire a different sort
of organisation, sensibility and life? By heat. And what will produce
the heat? Movement . . . (PH 274-5)

Of course there are great unanswered questions here. Diderot
addresses himself in particular to the question of the unity of
the sentient being. How can all the different molecules which
make up a chicken or a philosopher act as one being? How does
contiguity become continuity? The difficulty of such problems
is indicated by the fact that Diderot's answers consist partly of
analogies – with a swarm of bees, a monastery or quicksilver.
As he himself says, quoting an older saying, 'comparison is not
reason', and the reader is probably left with a feeling that he has

56

not been taken very far towards a real understanding of such matters.

There are bound to be weaknesses in what is essentially an attempt to solve the problem of the origin of life, but it is important to see that the notion of universal sensibility, vague as it is, clears the way for an exploration of human behaviour and thought which does without the mysterious notion of soul or spirit. In the second dialogue of *D'Alembert's Dream*, Diderot introduces a doctor, Bordeu (a famous doctor in real life), who goes a lot further in the detailed explanation of the way the human body and mind work. He talks about the interrelation of the different parts of the body, the functioning of the nervous system, the role of the brain, the physical causes of various forms of pathological behaviour, the operation of memory and many other matters. The essential point to emerge is that for Bordeu (and he convinces his interlocutor, Mademoiselle de Lespinasse) each individual's personality is above all the result of his or her biological make-up. For Diderot, as for Locke, all our ideas do indeed originate in the senses, but our mental operations, our intelligence or dullness, sensitivity or insensitivity, depend primarily on the state of what he calls our 'fibres', which may broadly be equated with the nervous system.

It is noteworthy that Diderot (through Bordeu) seeks to demonstrate this thesis quite largely by way of exceptional cases, what the period called 'monsters'. We saw in the previous chapter how the existence of 'monsters' (for example, the blind) can upset a belief in a comfortably ordered universe; here we observe that the exception can also serve to reveal the real physical laws that govern us. In *The Nun* the strange behaviour of women in a convent is meant to show something about the natural reaction of human beings to different environments; so here the stories of Siamese twins and the like bring out more clearly the dependence of mental states on bodily conditions.

All well and good, but what use are these ancient speculations to a present-day reader? The basic philosophical question of the nature of mind remains an open one, of course, but I doubt if there is much to interest a modern biologist or doctor in *D'Alembert's Dream*. The historian of scientific ideas will obviously find more in it; Diderot was not an isolated pioneer, but he was in the forefront of new thinking about man's place in the natural order. However, what most modern readers can derive from these dialogues is above all the feeling of expansive excitement as Diderot pursues all kinds of ideas, throwing out wild suggestions and analogies and miming in the form of his work his dynamic vision of the universe. It is not only a set of dialogues, it also contains a dream. In the sequences of the second dialogue which record d'Alembert's supposed dream, Diderot pushes his ideas to the limit, expanding his materialist account of man and the animals to a great vision of cosmic change. It is here above all that we see how far he has moved from the reassuring and majestic harmony of the Newtonian world system. Like Saunderson in the *Letter on the Blind*, the sleeping d'Alembert envisages Nature in a state of constant flux, where there is no longer any fixity of species:

Who knows what species of animals preceded us? And who knows what species of animals will follow ours? Everything changes, everything passes, only the All remains . . . (PH 299–300)

The miracle is life and sensibility, and this miracle is no longer a miracle . . . When once I have seen inert matter pass into a sensitive state, nothing can astonish me. (PH 303)

Nothing is surprising, all is possible. And indeed this section of the work is full of heady speculations about the origin and development of species. Diderot is a long way removed from Darwin's teleological notion of natural selection, but there are moments when he seems to hint at the scheme of evolution which was later developed by Lamarck. Take for instance the remark thrown out by Bordeu: 'Our organs produce our needs, and conversely our needs produce our organs' (PH 308). This is a strikingly bold statement in an age when most people believed – and were expected to believe – that the different parts of creation always had been, and would always remain, what they are now.

Through the dreaming d'Alembert, whose words are explicated by the sober Bordeu, Diderot thus paints a vivid picture of a cosmos of matter in constant movement, a vision of universal flux which is both stimulating and frightening. It must be stressed, however, that this is still an ordered world. It is subject to physical laws and to the overriding law of cause and effect. Nowhere in Diderot do we find anything like his contemporary Hume's critique of causality. On the contrary, he declares that we live in and are part of a material world whose laws govern all our actions and all our thoughts. Like Freud over a century later, he combines a view of man which is profoundly disturbing to habitual ways of thinking with the scientist's insistence that all the phenomena he is describing have the regularity (and thus, if we knew enough, the predictability) of the laws of matter.

Determinism is therefore a recurrent theme in his thinking. As early as 1756, in a celebrated letter to the playwright Landois, Diderot explains his views in these terms:

The word *freedom* has no meaning; there are and there can be no free beings; we are simply the product of the general order of things, our physical organisation, our education and the chain of events. These things exert an irresistible influence over us. One can no more conceive of a being behaving without a motive than of one arm of a scales moving up or down without the action of a weight. (C I 213)

This was not necessarily a comfortable view for a man with a warm attachment to the idea of virtue, since as he says in the letter to Landois and again in *D'Alembert's Dream*, vice and virtue are also empty words (in that they imply an idea of personal responsibility) and should be replaced in a philosophical vocabulary by the terms 'beneficence' and 'maleficence'. Men and women cannot be rationally punished or rewarded for a free exercise of will, but they can be 'modified' by praise, blame, laws, examples, rewards and punishments (and presumably brain surgery and the like). Of course in his turn the 'modifier' is no more free than the person modified. Diderot is facing here the issue raised in Marx's third thesis on Feuerbach: 'The materialist doctrine concerning the changing of circumstances and education forgets that the circumstances must be changed by people, and that the educator must himself be educated.' In fact, in his later writing, Diderot puts forward a more complex idea of determinism than that proposed in the letter to Landois, and suggests that the well-organised person, the *philosophe* for instance, may be capable of self-modification. He also makes fun of the whole intractable question in his novel *Jacques the Fatalist*. Here the hero repeats parrot-like his former master's lessons of fatalism, but still manages to act resourcefully and (for those about him) unpredictably. Determinism, though it may seem at odds with our normal perceptions, provides a comfortable and unconstraining framework for ordinary life.

At all events, the postulate of physical determinism was essential to Diderot's philosophical and scientific vision. As I have said, he envisaged a natural world (including man) in a state of constant though law-governed change, which scientists will gradually come to understand more fully. But what is the relation between this complex and dynamic order of nature and the ordered systems which men and women create in the fields of morals, politics or aesthetics.? If we rule out the possibility that there are God-given laws which can govern our behaviour, can we hope to find a solid foundation for our laws in nature? What reason have we to think that nature is on our side? These are questions which taxed Diderot in his mature years, unanswerable questions it may be said, and questions which remain unanswered, yet difficult to ignore.

At one extreme there is the awareness that 'vice and virtue, everything is equally in nature' (PH 507), or, in Dostoevsky's words, 'if God does not exist, everything is permitted.' Diderot approached this position at times but, as with his contemporaries, his dearest wish was to root his own moral and aesthetic values securely in a natural order. From first to last nature was one of his key words. It figures in two of his titles, *Thoughts on the Interpretation of Nature*, where it stands for the natural world, and *The Natural Son*, where it draws our attention both to the artificiality of French marriage laws and to the 'natural' virtues in which all the characters are finally and happily united. What then does Diderot mean by natural morality?

An article entitled 'Natural Law', which appeared in the *Encyclopedia* in 1755, spells out more clearly the idea of a law of nature which can underpin a satisfactory social code. Diderot takes up the traditional debate against pessimistic thinkers such as Hobbes. The challenge which he has to answer is that of the violent man (an ancestor of the marquis de Sade), who speaks in the following terms:

I realise that I am carrying terror and disorder into the midst of the human species; but either I must be unhappy or I must cause unhappiness for others, and no one is dearer to me than I am to myself. Let no one blame me for this hateful predilection; I am not free to be otherwise. The voice of nature never expresses itself more strongly within me than when it speaks in favour of myself. (P 31)

Diderot's answer to this lies in an appeal to a 'general will' which is 'always good'. This is not Rousseau's political

61

'general will' which is confined to one particular community; this article expresses a belief in the general agreement of all human beings on a universally valid moral code:

It is your conformity with all other men and their conformity with you which will indicate to you when you are parting company with your species and when you are remaining within it. Never lose sight of it therefore, or you will see the notions of goodness, justice, humanity and virtue begin to crumble in your mind. Say to yourself frequently: 'I am a man, and I have no other truly inalienable rights than those of humanity.' (P 33)

'I am a man' seems to refer to the famous dictum of Terence: 'I am a man and I do not regard anything human as foreign to me.' This universalism never left Diderot; he shared it with many of his contemporaries, though not with Rousseau, whose political ideal of citizenship was at odds with the cosmopolitanism of many of his former friends. It may seem to contradict the evolutionary vision of *D'Alembert's Dream*, but Diderot explains in 'Natural Law' that 'even if one were to suppose the notion of species in a state of constant flux, the nature of *natural law* would not change because it will always be relative to the general will and the common wishes of the whole species' (P 34). At any time, therefore, one might hope to draw up a natural code based on the general consent of all peoples, a set of laws which are always found to lead to the greater happiness of the individual and the species.

For of course the ultimate criterion of this code of nature is happiness. Diderot does not propose the sort of calculation of relative sums of happiness which we find in utilitarian moral thought, but he certainly sees no other justification for virtuous behaviour than that it will increase happiness. This will even be true when the individual sacrifices his or her selfish interests, since nature has conveniently installed in us all a moral sense which will make us unhappy if we ignore it (what

Diderot's Scottish contemporary Adam Smith called the 'impartial spectator'). This is how the heroine Constance preaches to the hero Dorval in *The Natural Son*:

The effect of virtue on our souls is no less necessary and no less powerful than that of beauty on our senses . . . in the heart of man there is a taste for order which is older than any process of reflective thought . . . it is this taste which makes us susceptible to shame, and it is shame which makes us fear contempt more even than death. (O X 64)

In this way nature acts as a moral policeman. Just as excessive drinking or debauchery brings illness, so anti-social behaviour will bring us the unhappiness that comes from knowing that we seem despicable to others. It is this natural moral order which gives us the strength to act virtuously in the face of ridicule and apparent unhappiness. Quite late in life, in the *Refutation of Helvétius*, Diderot declared yet again, as he had at various stages throughout his career:

Even in a society as badly ordered as ours, when successful vice is often applauded and unsuccessful virtue almost always ridiculed, I am convinced that in the last analysis our best way to happiness is to act virtuously. (PH 595)

In a 'badly ordered' society this is an act of faith. It would be better of course if society could be ordered more in accordance with the laws of nature. In the *Supplement to Bougainville's Voyage* and elsewhere, Diderot puts forward the idea of the 'three codes', the code of nature, the civil code and the religious code. These are almost always at odds in society. Inevitably, therefore, people are torn between different duties, whereas ideally we should either dispense with the two man-made codes or bring them into line with the code of nature.

But what is this elusive set of rules? It is all very well to use

63

words like goodness, justice or humanity – we are all in favour of virtue. But can such words be given any positive content? Very often it seems, as the previous chapter suggested, that the idea of nature is an essentially *critical* one. The vague notion of natural goodness serves to throw into sharper relief the follies of existing society. Thus in Diderot's novels *Jacques the Fatalist* and *The Nun*, in such stories as *This is not a Story* or *Madame de la Carlière* and in the *Conversation of a Father with his Children* various misfortunes are seen as the result of the clash between natural morality and the laws or customs of society. The *Conversation*, for instance, raises the question: is a wise man justified in breaking an unjust law? The discussion turns on a series of anecdotes. Of these the most striking concerns the finding of an old will which seems to deprive the rightful and poverty-stricken inheritors of a small fortune in favour of a rich and apparently undeserving man. Should the person who finds the will burn it? Diderot, who appears as a character in this conversation piece, has no doubt that he should, because 'the reason of the human species is far more sacred than the reason of a legislator.' On the other hand, the philosopher's firm statement is equally firmly rejected by his father, and we cannot take the character 'Myself' as speaking unequivocally for the author. But in any case it is evident that bad laws cause unhappiness.

It is interesting to note that a work entitled the *Code of Nature* by Morelly was attributed by contemporaries to Diderot and even figured in the first collected edition of his works. It puts forward an alarmingly regimented utopian social organisation. It is odd that this should have been thought of as his work, since, with its deathly rigidity, it seems precisely the sort of work he could not have written. Nor is there anything in his writings like Rousseau's *Émile*, which outlines stage by stage an upbringing supposedly in accordance with the laws of nature. However, in certain of his later writings, Diderot does paint some rapid sketches of a better social order. Writing for Catherine of Russia, for instance, he speaks of the need for a nation to have a written code, a 'uniform and general law'(P 224). He also suggests the sort of reforms which in any country would bring about greater general happiness: reduction of the power and wealth of the church, greater fairness in the distribution of the tax burden, removal of unjustified privileges, rewards for merit and virtue, reform of the penal code and so on. Likewise, in his contributions to Raynal's *History of the Two Indies* we can see the expression of a more rational approach to legislation and social organisation. There is nothing very remarkable about all this; Diderot shares the liberal reformist position of many of his contemporaries, appealing like them to a universal (and therefore natural) standard of reason, though tempering it to suit the situation of particular countries.

The order of nature is most directly invoked in Diderot's most utopian work, the *Supplement to Bougainville's Voyage*. As we have seen, this is by no means a straightforward work, and the utopian element in it is framed by conversations that show it to be a dream rather than a blueprint for reform. The main thrust of the dialogue is satirical, but the satire rests on a vision of a more 'natural' organisation of sexual, family and social life. Diderot's Tahiti is a society with a minimum of laws, not a society without laws. For instance, because nature invites men and women to mate so as to perpetuate the species, there are in this earthly paradise no rules enjoining marital fidelity, and children are regarded as the common wealth of the whole community. There are however rules against unproductive sexual practices – dissolute women who continue to receive men after they have passed the age of childbearing are exiled to another part of the island. None of this is very ferocious perhaps, but it shows that nature can provide a sanction for repression – and incidentally that the laws of Diderot's nature are aligned with the concern for increasing the birth-rate which was common among the *philosophes*, and which has persisted in France to the present day.

The final conversation of the *Supplement* makes it clear that the establishment of a natural code of sexuality is no easy matter for members of an advanced society. The speaker 'B', who seems most to represent Diderot, says, 'I should be inclined to think that the most savage people on earth, the Tahitians, who have kept scrupulously to the law of nature, are nearer to a good system of laws than any civilised people' (PH 505). Similar remarks are to be found in his writings for Raynal. The editor of the *Encyclopedia*, like several of his friends and acquaintances, had a considerable streak of primitivism, and this became stronger as he grew older. Committed though he was to technical and scientific progress and to the cause of rational thought, he also looked nostalgically to the simpler, nobler and happier world of the savage, the Ancients and even – at times – the peasant. One of his stories, *The Two Friends of Bourbonne* (*Les Deux Amis de Bourbonne*), shows the sublime friendship of two simple country people and contrasts it favourably with the civilised inhumanity and folly of judges, landowners and priests. Such notions remained pretty theoretical of course, but they kept alive the faith that a better moral and social order might be found.

The theme of the 'noble savage' is only one aspect of the search for universally valid systems with which this chapter has been concerned. I have concentrated on scientific and moral questions, but we may rapidly note the same universalising urge at work in two other fields, aesthetics and language.

In the speech from *The Natural Son* quoted above, the moral sense is compared to the sense of beauty that is shared by all men and women. In thinking about beauty Diderot was torn between a relativist awareness of the difference of tastes ('there is no disputing about tastes') and the familiar desire to find what David Hume called the 'standard of taste', some generally applicable criterion of beauty. In his *Discourse on Dramatic Poetry* he wrote:

It is certain that there will be no end to our disputes as long as each person takes himself as model and judge. There will be as many standards as there are individuals, and for each individual there will be as many different standards as there are different periods in his life.

That is enough, I think, to show the necessity of seeking for a standard which is not peculiar to me. Until this is done most of my judgements will be wrong and all of them will be insecure. (E 284)

Between his translation of Shaftesbury of 1745 and his last art criticism of the 1770s, he puzzled over this problem, seeking always to overcome the chaos of mere subjectivism. Corresponding to the *Encyclopedia* article 'Natural Law' there is the article entitled 'Beauty' (*Beau*). This contains an attempt to found the idea of beauty on the abstract notion of 'relationships'. The notion is so general as to be virtually meaningless, but only through this degree of generality can Diderot preserve the idea of a beauty which does not depend on particular perceptions. Thus he is able to reach the reassuring if hollow conclusion that 'Whatever may be the causes of the diversity of our judgements, this is not a reason for believing that real beauty, the beauty that consists in the perception of relationships, is merely a figment of the imagination' (E 435).

The *Encyclopedia* article is hardly satisfactory. It is likely to reveal to the modern reader simply an excessive faith in the power of reason to account for beauty. In this faith Diderot was a man of his time; indeed, in some respects he holds to ideas about art which were derived from the French classical

67

period, if not earlier. In later years, as he acquired a much greater practical knowledge of many of the arts, he did not abandon the belief that beauty exists in reality and not just in the eye of the beholder. Now, however, he was more inclined to situate it in the 'imitation of nature'. But of course the word 'nature' once again raises all kinds of problems: above all, is the nature to be imitated an ideal nature or the nature of *D'Alembert's Dream*? I shall return to this question in the final chapter.

Diderot's thinking about language exhibits the same uncertain belief in a universally valid order. The eighteenth century was the golden age of 'general grammar'. Philosophical grammarians tried to describe the fundamental structure which underpinned the variety of actual languages, a structure which was supposed to correspond to the processes of human thought, since these were everywhere the same. At one point in his *Letter on the Deaf and Dumb* (which includes some of his most interesting remarks on language and art) Diderot declares that Cicero, before speaking his sentences in their Latin order must have thought them in their logical French order (subject – verb – predicate). It is not surprising therefore that he, like Leibniz or Condillac, toyed with the dream of a universal language which would represent the natural world as it impinges on the mind of human beings:

Once such a language was accepted and established, our ideas would become permanent, distant times and places would come together, links would be set up between every inhabited point in space and time and all living and thinking beings would be able to communicate. (O VII 189)

But again this universal order is a dream rather than an attainable reality. Diderot speaks elsewhere of his 'well-founded habit of suspecting all general laws concerning language'

(O VII 194). In observing language, as in observing life, he was too conscious of multiplicity to be an untroubled apostle of universal order. He wanted order and laws, and up to a point he found them or created them, but he also saw variety and exceptions.

6 The exception and the rule – *Rameau's Nephew*

Diderot was strongly drawn to universal systems of science, ethics and aesthetics, but as I have suggested in the last chapter, he could not rest securely in any of the orders he created. He was too keenly aware of the diversity of things, which gives the lie to such explanatory schemes. And it is this above all which gives Diderot's writing its abiding value. As a free-thinker and as the propounder of a new order he is in the mainstream of Enlightenment thought, even though the scope of his critical and constructive thinking often puts him at the radical edge of the movement. What is most remarkable about him is the constant interplay between ordered systems and order-breaking facts, between unity and multiplicity, between the rule and the exception.

The dialogue *Rameau's Nephew* is the work of Diderot's which displays most powerfully this openness to aspects of reality that fly in the face of his own desire for order. It is his best and most challenging piece of writing, and stands at the centre of his work; I am therefore devoting this chapter mainly to a more detailed account of this dialogue than I have given of any of his other books. But first I should like to say a few words about certain other writings which display the same sort of interest in the exception that breaks the rule.

What we are concerned with here is the importance for Diderot of the particular fact. He wrote in his *Thoughts on the Interpretation of Nature*: 'Facts, of whatever kind, constitute the philosopher's true wealth' (PH 191). The world of facts had confronted him above all in his work as *encyclopédiste*, where as general editor he had been responsible for articles on all kinds of subjects. In particular, he attached great importance to the technological side of the work. The *Encyclopedia* is full of *things*; the twelve volumes of plates display in detail the material labour of French society. It appears moreover that the editor often made a point of getting his informants to show him the practical operation of the machines which are described and depicted in text and plates. Similarly, as he turned from the abstractions of mathematics and metaphysics to natural science, he sought information from the most advanced practitioners. And as an art critic too, having originally approached pictures in a literary, non-technical way, he profited from the guidance of practising artists, who initiated him into the details of their profession. Again and again in Diderot, for all his expansive elaboration of hypotheses, we see this thirst for the concrete, this taste for the particular. And it was inevitable that this tendency should sometimes come into conflict with the larger orders towards which we saw him working in the last chapter.

A good example of his attachment to the real, as against abstract theory, is to be found in his *Apology for the Abbé Galiani*. In 1767 he had been bowled over by the all-explaining economic doctrines of the Physiocrats, as expounded for instance in a work with the alluring title *The Essential Order* (by Mercier de la Rivière). But under the influence of his cynical Italian friend Galiani he came to doubt the practical value of the Physiocrats' teaching that there should be complete freedom in the importing and exporting of grain. Above all, on a visit to the Langres area in 1770, he saw something of the havoc caused by free trade, and wrote the *Apology* as a fierce attack on the defender of the doctrine, the abbé Morellet. He pours scorn on Morellet's 'general principles', all of which are subject to 'an infinite number of objections in practice'. Morellet is merely an abstract reasoner: 'A metaphysician feeding on abstract ideas in his study will never have the professional's feel for his material. To speak to any purpose about baking, you need to have had your hands in dough' (P 70). In particular the Physiocrats' principles had led them to neglect the real suffering of the poor in the famines of 1768; so that Diderot's defence of empiricism is also a defence of humanity. Given the intractability of such economic and political problems it is small wonder that a short time after, in his *Refutation of Helvétius*, he includes free trade in a list of great and insoluble questions, the very questions of course which most attracted him.

In the *Refutation of Helvétius* one sees the critique of system-building in a quite different field, that of psychology. Claude-Adrien Helvétius (1715–71) was an enthusiastic member of the *philosophe* party. His first major book, *On Mind (De l'esprit)*, had been condemned for materialism in 1758, along with the *Encyclopedia*. In 1771 a posthumous sequel, *On Man*, appeared; here Helvétius spelled out once again his explanation of human behaviour and thought. Essentially, in his view, human beings of 'normal constitution' are all potentially capable of anything; we all possess the same fundamental desire for pleasure and aversion to pain, and all the distinctions between us are to be explained by the different sense impressions which we have received since the time of our birth. Thus the way is open, as in certain modern behaviourist theories, for educators and legislators to form and deform the human personality for the greater good of all.

Diderot approved of the general thrust of Helvétius's argument, his attack on innate ideas and his call for rational reform. But he found himself unable to accept many of his more sweeping statements. He points to the flaws in Helvétius's over-simplification of human psychology: while our sensations may be the necessary *condition* for us to make judgements, they do not in themselves constitute judgement, something else is needed; and while personal interest certainly acts as a spur to action, it is an unwarranted short-cut to say that the desire for physical pleasure is at the root of all the acts of heroism and self-sacrifice which Diderot so admired. In all this, he pleads the case for human complexity against the hasty over-simplifications of his philosophical ally. In particular, again and again, he stresses the difference between one person and another. Characteristically, he gives examples from his own life. For all his desire to succeed with women, he could never learn to dance properly. Similarly he is prevented by nature from producing the work of genius that he admires in certain poets. Helvétius says that a 'powerful motive' is enough to make anyone capable of anything, but Diderot replies that if he were put in the Bastille and given ten years to write a scene worthy of Racine or be executed, he might as well be executed straight away.

It should not be thought that he is here going back on the materialistic theory of mind of *D'Alembert's Dream*. He still believes in the ultimate possibility of a scientific explanation of human thought and behaviour, without recourse to the idea of soul or spirit. But he is far more aware than Helvétius of the importance of our physical organisation. Just as for a materialist we are differentiated from the animals by our different physical make-up, so for Diderot one person is different from another not just through the chances of upbringing, but because of differences in the body, the brain, the nervous system and so on. It is this which gives us what he calls an 'innate aptitude' for one thing rather than another. This is what explains the existence of geniuses and eccentrics: 'In my view an *eccentric* [*un original*] is a strange being who derives his extraordinary way of seeing, feeling and expressing himself from his character' (PH 578). It will be explained later in the work that this 'character' depends primarily on the 'two main-springs of the machine', the brain, which determines our mental powers, and the diaphragm, which Diderot sees as the seat of human emotivity.

Once again we return to the theme of the 'monster'. This name is given to creatures whose physical make-up is distinctly abnormal, but in a sense we are all monsters, or rather each person is constituted differently from all the rest. It is this diversity, this monstrosity, that clearly fascinated Diderot when he observed the human world. This was what attracted him in the history, literature and art of the past, and this was what he liked to show in his portrayals of the modern world. His fiction is full of strange individuals. There is the heartless 'monster' or 'tiger' Gardeil in the short story called *This is not a Story*. There are the various deranged women who figure in the dark and melodramatic pages of *The Nun*. Above all in *Jacques the Fatalist* there is a whole gallery of eccentrics, from the two officers who cannot stop duelling together to the remarkably cool villain, Father Hudson. Almost always these unusual beings are monsters of depravity, if looked at from the standpoint of conventional morality, or indeed from Diderot's own position as a public-spirited *philosophe*. Sometimes (as in *The Nun*) he can assign their strange behaviour to their environment. More often they appear as puzzles, interesting, perhaps attractive, and irreducible to any simple and satisfactory moral system. This is what happens in the work which is arguably the high point of Diderot's imaginative writing, *Rameau's Nephew*.

Rameau's Nephew is a relatively short work in dialogue form, described as a 'satire' and begun about 1761, in the dark period of Diderot's life after the suppression of the *Encyclopedia*. He kept it to himself for the rest of his life, never mentioning it in any surviving texts, modifying and enlarging it, and leaving after his death a carefully written manuscript, which seems to indicate how important it was to him. And indeed it can fairly be seen as the very centre of his writing. As such, over two centuries it has attracted a vast body of commentary, from the translation of an enthusiastic Goethe, where it first appeared in print, to the many exegetic volumes of modern scholarship and criticism.

There are two people in the dialogue, a philosopher called 'Myself', who can indeed be identified with certain sides of the author, and a musician called Rameau, the nephew of the famous composer. Rameau, while being a person in his own right, also embodies certain aspects of Diderot. In addition we hear the voice of a narrator who introduces the conversation and periodically comments on the behaviour of Rameau and the reactions of the philosopher. Clearly the narrator is very close to 'Myself', but he is not quite the same person, since he is looking back on the dialogue from a later point in time. This enables the author to keep a distance between himself and what he is showing.

Although many 'philosophical' issues are discussed in *Rameau's Nephew*, it is not so much a philosophical dialogue in the manner of Plato or Hume as a quasi-dramatic representation of the confrontation of two figures and their changing relationship. At the outset the narrator-philosopher is clearly in command; he is the detached observer who watches the world go by, as he watches the chess-players of the Café de la Régence in the Palais Royal gardens. Later he too will become involved in the chess game. When Rameau appears, he is presented as an unusual phenomenon, worthy of the philosopher's attention. Like the blind man, the deranged nun or the monster, he will help the thinker to achieve a more complete picture of reality. This doesn't mean, however, that he is to be taken as the philosopher's equal:

I have no great regard for such eccentrics; others make companions or even friends of them. They detain me once in a year, when I happen to come across them, because their character stands out against all the rest, and they disrupt the tedious uniformity which our education, our social conventions and our manners have introduced among us. (R 425)

The 'once in a year' suggests that this is to be a kind of Saturnalia, a brief period of licensed folly interrupting the regular order of things. Thinking people use such occasions to discover the truth.

In accordance with this programme, 'Myself' questions Rameau in such a way as to bring out his individuality. The dialogue and the narrative paint a vivid picture of a remarkable man. He appears as the anti-*philosophe*, glorying in what 'Myself' regards as his immorality. He is an accomplished musical performer, but knowing that he lacks the genius of his uncle, he chooses to make a living by exploiting the vices and follies of society. In particular he exists as a parasite in the house of the financier Bertin (a real-life individual), for whom he performs all sorts of useful and degrading functions – flatterer, buffoon, pimp and leader of the claque which applauds the feeble efforts of Bertin's actress-mistress. As such he is an unflattering representation of Diderot's adversaries in the troubled years around 1760; seen from one angle the work is a fierce and vindictive satire, a condemnation of those who were content to swim with the tide, siding with the powerful against the *philosophes* – a partisan view, needless to say.

However, Rameau is not simply presented as someone to be condemned, nor even as a mere catalyst who will help the philosopher to a more complete knowledge of humanity. 'Myself' and the narrator may look on him with superior condescension at the beginning of the dialogue, but he quickly asserts himself as a person to be reckoned with, so much so that many readers (Hegel being the most notable) have seen in him the destroyer of the false 'good conscience' of the *philosophe* – of the bourgeois too perhaps. For one thing, he is a force of nature. Not only is he a 'compound of dignity and baseness, of good sense and unreason', he is also gifted with 'a powerful organism, a singularly ardent imagination and an unusually strong pair of lungs' (R 424). As well as being a musician, he is a remarkable mimic, and the narrator re-creates in words some of his extraordinary performances. He plays the different parts in imaginary sonatas, operas or symphonies, attracting the attention of all bystanders and arousing in 'Myself' a mixture of admiration, pity and amusement. Or else he acts brief scenes, comic and immoral sketches from life as he knows it. Or again he tells stories, with great cynical verve, and at a crucial point in the dialogue he manages to shock and confuse his narrator with his tale of the Renegade of Avignon.

The Renegade is a total villain; he swindles his Jewish protector out of his fortune and denounces him to the Inquisition to be burnt at the stake. Rameau concludes his dreadful story with the blackly ironic flourish: 'And thus it was that the renegade entered into the untroubled possession of the fortune of this accursed descendant of those who crucified our Lord.' 'Myself' exclaims: 'I do not know which horrifies me most, the villainy of your renegade or your tone in talking about him.' Whereupon Rameau can declare triumphantly:

Just as I said. The atrocity of the act carries you beyond contempt, and that is why I am sincere [in confessing my vices]. I wanted you to know how I excel in my art, to force you to confess that at least I am original in my degradation, to place myself in your mind in the line of the great scoundrels . . . (R 489–90)

and he bursts into a fugal chorus to Molière's words 'Vivat Mascarillus, fourbum imperator', a song of praise to himself

77

as a sublime comic artist. In other words, Rameau asks 'Myself' to 'discuss a horrible deed, an abominable crime, as a connoisseur of painting and poetry examines the beauties of a work of art'. He is presented as someone with a strong aesthetic sense, and indeed he gives the philosopher lessons in musical appreciation, expounding a theory of beauty which Diderot himself held. What matters to him is a certain notion of sublimity, of successful performance, and he has no time for his interlocutor's altruistic moral beliefs. Quite early in the dialogue, taking the initiative, he questions 'Myself' about his daughter's education (Diderot's daughter Angélique was eight years old in 1761). Against the normal lessons in music and dancing (Angélique did in fact become a gifted harpsichordist), the philosopher sets an education which is intellectual and above all moral, but Rameau retorts: 'How easy it would be for me to prove to you the uselessness of all that knowledge in a world such as ours; it is worse than useless, it is positively dangerous' (R 449). Likewise, when the *philosophe*, representing the ideal natural order, talks of the pleasures of virtuous self-sacrifice, Rameau looks on in amazement. Patriotism, friendship, family affection and public spirit are mere vanity to him. And when challenged on the immorality of certain of his actions (his tricks of the trade as a music teacher, for instance) he in his turn challenges the validity of the principles by which he is being judged:

I know quite well that if you go applying [to my actions] certain general principles of some strange morality that everyone talks about but no one practises, it will turn out that black is white and white is black. But, my dear philosopher, there is a general conscience, just as there is a general grammar, with exceptions in every language . . . (R 453)

The comparison with language is revealing. Rameau defends the exception against the rule – or rather he suggests that the exception *is* the rule. Any attempt to set up a universally valid code of morality is thus as pointless as attempts to find universal principles of language. In 'a world such as ours' his behaviour seems natural and productive of greater pleasure for all; so-called virtue is cold and unlovable, so-called vice is what makes the world go round.

But what about conscience, what about the general will of which Diderot speaks in the article 'Natural Law'? Rameau declares that he is blind and deaf to such promptings. Vice comes naturally to him. How then is one to explain this lack of a moral sense which is supposedly part of our natural equipment for living? Rameau suggests two answers, both of them consonant with a materialist view of human nature. The first stresses environment, along the lines suggested by Helvétius: 'Perhaps it is because I have always lived with good musicians and wicked people' (R 501). In accordance with this, he brings up his son to follow his example:

Instead of stuffing his head with fine maxims that he would only have to forget unless he wants to finish up a beggar, I place myself in front of him whenever I have a piece of gold (which is not often), I take the gold out of my pocket, I show it to him with signs of admiration, I kiss it and lift my eyes to heaven . . . (R 503)

But all of this would be to no avail if the boy was not born, like his father, with the appropriate character, and as in the *Refutation of Helvétius* this is seen to depend on his physical make-up, described here in terms of 'fibres' and the 'paternal molecule'. If Rameau is 'insensitive to the charms of virtue', it is because there is 'a fibre which I did not receive, or a slack fibre which fails to vibrate however much it is plucked' (R 501). As he sees it, he is properly equipped by nature for the sort of life he leads.

Now Diderot in his thinking about vice, virtue and the public good was persuaded that some individuals are 'badly

born', predestined by forces beyond their control to act crimi-
nally. Such people cannot in his view be blamed, but they can
be 'modified', by education, legislation, encouragement,
reward or punishment. In this way, as 'Myself' says in
Rameau's Nephew, it may be possible to 'counteract the influence of the paternal molecule'. If this fails, says Diderot in his
1756 letter to Landois, then society will have to 'destroy the
evil-doer in the public square'.

So is Rameau a candidate for modification or liquidation?
Certainly there are moments in the dialogue when the philosopher expresses himself quite violently about the vices of
his contemporaries. Pimps deserved to be thrashed, he
says – but Rameau replies with the sort of ironical superiority
that 'Myself' had used on him: 'Thrashed, sir! Thrashed!
There is no thrashing in a well-ordered society' (R 432). For
the strong point of his challenge to the so-called natural order
of the Enlightenment philosopher is not so much that he has
quite different values (more or less the values of the rogue-
hero of the picaresque tradition) as that the values he represents are now seen as the norm rather than the exception. His
ideal of happiness is one of anti-social self-indulgence, and
when the philosopher tells him sarcastically that this way of
life would be 'highly honourable to the human race, highly
useful to your fellow-citizens and highly conducive to your
own reputation', he has an easy and apparently victorious
riposte:

I do believe you are mocking me; my dear philosopher, you don't
know who you are taking on; you don't realise that at this moment I
represent the majority of the court and city. Our wealthy people in all
walks of life may or may not have said to themselves what I have said
to you, but in any case the life I would lead is precisely the one they
lead. That's how you people are. You think the same sort of happiness suits everyone. What an extraordinary idea! Your kind of

happiness needs a certain romantic turn of mind which we don't share, an unusual soul and a peculiar taste. You give the name of virtue to this oddity; you call it philosophy. (R 456)

It must be remembered that Diderot began *Rameau's Nephew* at a time when he felt himself the victim of persecution. His vision of French society is therefore blacker in this work than it is for instance in his optimistic plays. But in any case it is striking that the decent *philosophe*, who is a figure of respectable normality as he examines his odd acquaintance at the beginning of the dialogue, comes to look more like the odd man out by the end. Rameau plays the part of the fool, but in doing so, like the traditional jester, he turns the tables by casting doubts on the sanity of those who patronise him. If one is to believe him, it is 'Myself' who is setting himself against the great order of nature, in which the strong prey on the weak.

The reversal is neatly brought out by references to Diogenes, the Greek Cynic philosopher who incarnated the refusal of civilised society (and whom some contemporaries saw reincarnated in Jean-Jacques Rousseau, who was always an important point of reference for Diderot). In the opening pages of the dialogue, it is Rameau who mockingly compares himself to Diogenes in reply to the condescension of 'Myself'; at the end, driven into a corner by his interlocutor's corrosive cynicism, it is the philosopher who puts forward Diogenes as a model. At this stage the two speakers have reached a vision of the world as a gigantic pantomime where everyone is forced to bow and scrape to someone else, but 'Myself' claims that there is one person who remains exempt from this, the philosopher, who can if need be shake off the false demands of civilisation and live on berries and roots: 'May I be struck dead if that would not be better than crawling, debasing yourself and prostituting yourself' (R 517).

This eloquent last stand is hardly convincing, however much it may have corresponded to Diderot's own beliefs when he wrote it. Certainly it means nothing to Rameau, who after a last comic turn strolls off to watch the opera. And the work finishes on an enigmatic proverb, the French equivalent of 'He who laughs last, laughs best.' But who does laugh best? Neither side can really be said to 'win' an argument where there is so little common ground. Rameau can claim that his way of life and his values suit him and fit in with his society, and that to act 'virtuously' would be a pointless and hypocritical distortion of his true self. 'Myself', on the other hand, looking beyond the present, can place his hope in the future of humanity. He may be the odd man out in Rameau's world, but the odd man out can also be seen as the pioneer. In an important section early on in the dialogue, the two men talk about genius. Rameau, perhaps out of envy, regards the genius as a trouble-maker, but the philosopher defends him in the name of the 'good of the species'. Like the genius, the virtuous man serves humanity as a whole. And in addition he claims (as Diderot kept claiming throughout his life) that the virtuous individual enjoys a more genuine and durable happiness. Where Rameau, dependent on everything around him, oscillates according to the circumstances of the moment, 'Myself' stands for the stability of the self-sufficient wise man.

In their dispute, both speakers invoke nature. They are referring to two different conceptions of nature, of which Rameau's is possibly the one that is now more prevalent. And indeed the musician, to whom the moral strenuousness of 'Myself' is quite foreign, might at first seem the more 'natural' of the two. He himself says that he can achieve happiness through vices that come naturally to him, and that he is simply observing the 'universal and sacred pact' of a nature in which all creatures live off one another. He fits without effort into a value-free universe. Yet even this is not true; his weak point is that in spite of himself he feels the need for a sort of dignity. He has had to work on himself to become the supple performer that he is, just as it has taken practice and effort to render his naturally stiff hand flexible enough to play the violin. And just when he is doing well as a parasite, as at home in flattery as a fish in water, his dignity springs up like a jack-in-the-box and costs him his comfortable place.

In other words, nature provides no guarantee, no firm backing for any particular line of behaviour. 'Vices and virtues, everything is equally in nature' (PH 507). In the ideal Tahiti of the *Supplement to Bougainville's Voyage* it might be possible to live naturally and innocently, but in the society that Diderot knew no natural code seemed able to provide a reliable guide. Indeed one may ask whether the root of the trouble is not in this particular Paris-centred society, with its hierarchy and inequality. As Rameau says, with a bitterness which recalls the end of Rousseau's *Discourse on Inequality*, 'What a way of running things – some people with too much of everything, while others have stomachs that cry out and not a crust to eat' (R 154). His plight is that of one who is born poor into a world where wealth controls everything. It is no good the *philosophe* telling him that he should have 'found himself a livelihood independent of servitude' (the *Encyclopedia* perhaps?); such positions do not exist in his society, and it is for this reason that at the end even 'Myself' is driven to envisage a return to savage nature. *Rameau's Nephew* is confined to Paris, a place of corruption and rapid fortunes; it contains no glimpse of the steady world of Langres, let alone the Swiss paradises of Rousseau's books.

To put it in more modern terms, 'Myself' and Rameau are 'in situation'. They have not apparently chosen their environment any more than they have chosen their physical make-up. But in this situation where God is well and truly dead and nature cannot take his place as a source of value, they have their choices to make. It is for them, and for Diderot's readers, to weigh up the pros and cons of these different ways of living and thinking. Nor does determinism provide an alibi. Even if, as Diderot believes, our apparently free actions are in fact the necessary result of a complex and unknowable network of causes, we continue, like Jacques the fatalist, to choose our own course of action within this determinist framework and to expect such choices of others. *Rameau's Nephew* proposes no unequivocal solution, as is abundantly evident from the many different ways it has been read. Nor, I think, does it simply set two viewpoints calmly side by side, transcending their differences in an impassive work of art. On the contrary, the power of this dialogue comes from its continuing ability to challenge and disturb. It gives dramatic (and richly comic) form to a perplexity which inhabitants of modern urban society face every day of their lives.

In *Rameau's Nephew*, more than in any other of Diderot's writings, we see the *philosophe*'s awareness of a reality which refuses to be encompassed by the orderly schemes of philosophy. It should not be thought however that he was always as alive to the claims of the Other as he shows himself to be in this remarkable work. For all his encyclopedic curiosity, he was a member of a small élite in eighteenth-century French society and tended – like anyone else – to view the rest of the world through the spectacles of a limiting vision. When he says with Terence that he is a man and therefore nothing human is foreign to him, this universalist declaration may mean that everything else can be brought into line with his habits and preoccupations. In true classical style he says, writing of Richardson, that the human heart 'was, is and will always be the same'. Therefore when he translated fragments of James Macpherson's 'poems of Ossian' into French, he tidied them up in accordance with the norms of French classical eloquence and made them sound quite like his own versions of Homer (O XIII 276–82). Similarly he gave the old man of Tahiti (in the *Supplement*) a speech which recalls the orators of antiquity. The classical culture which he had begun to imbibe at his Jesuit college provided a convenient way of assimilating the foreign cultures which existed at the fringe of his real experience, whether in the wilds of America, in Russia or in the Caledonia of the Ossianic poems.

The difficulty of doing justice to strange modes of experience is perhaps most obvious when Diderot is dealing not with the bohemian Rameau (who is almost a demonic *alter ego*), but with the peasants who formed the great mass of the French population at this time. He was himself a provincial and occasionally uses snatches of his native *patois*, but he was always a townsman or city dweller. This does not mean that he was ignorant or disdainful of country life. On the contrary, as an *encyclopédiste* he was committed to upgrading the status of useful labour, and particularly of agriculture, the backbone of the nation, and to reducing the burdens which the *ancien régime* laid on it. But this did not alter the fact that, as a well-to-do provincial said in the early years of the Revolution (when some notice was being paid to the peasants), the *patois* they spoke and other aspects of their culture made them 'an isolated and separate caste, which does not communicate with the town'.

This is why, in reading the quite numerous passages which Diderot devotes to ordinary country people (unusually numerous for the literature of the time, be it said), one is conscious of a wide gulf between observer and observed.

Diderot recognises this in one place, writing of an attempt to use country language in polite poetry:

A poem where all these rustic expressions were used would often have the defect of being unintelligible or of lacking harmony, dignity and grace, since these expressions have not been shaped by good taste, worked and softened by daily use and presented to our ears tamed, ennobled by figurative associations and freed from the base accessory ideas of poverty, degradation and the coarseness of those who live in the country. (A V 240-1)

Realistically, he is accepting the decorum that ruled literature. And so, when he himself wrote on such subjects, he resorted to different forms of stylisation. On the one hand, there is the comic form, notably in the section towards the end of *Jacques the Fatalist* where the peasant hero is talking about his sexual initiation. In one way the country people we see are like the Tahitians of the *Supplement*, innocent, natural and happy — as opposed to the artificially depraved and tormented upper-class protagonists such as Madame de la Pommeraye in the same novel. On the other hand, Diderot's way of presenting Dame Marguerite, Dame Suzon and the humorously named Bigre (in English, something like Booger) make them look like children, entertaining, attractive perhaps, but not to be taken as seriously as Madame de la Pommeraye by an upper-class audience.

Alternatively, and here Diderot is more innovatory, the peasant may be stylised on the model of heroic antiquity. This happens in the striking tale *The Two Friends of Bourbonne*, a story of two outlaws who are presented in the very first sentence as a modern Orestes and Pylades. Just as the *Encyclopedia* wanted to revalue agriculture and other forms of useful work, so Diderot in *The Two Friends* is trying to show that 'greatness of soul and noble qualities are to be found in all walks of life and in all countries'. In fact, the noble Homeric simplicity of much of the narration and dialogue does not really ring true; the dominant impression is of the *distance* which separates the world of the heroes from that of the author and the narrators (the story is presented as the work of several story-tellers). This distance is particularly well exemplified in an encounter near the beginning of the tale; the narrator and her friends are taking the waters at Bourbonne:

One evening when we were going for our usual walk, we saw a tall woman standing in front of a cottage with four small children at her feet; her firm and sad countenance attracted our attention, and our attention caught hers. After a moment's silence, she said to us: Here are four little children, I am their mother, and I no longer have a husband. (R 810–11)

Here, it seems to me, there is a confrontation of two social groups across a gap that can only be partially bridged by the bookish sublimity of the tableau and the woman's simple words; the peasant family represents an otherness to which Diderot cannot give voice as successfully as he does to that of Rameau, but at least he does enable us to glimpse this meeting of two worlds.

Perhaps he could imagine a society which would bring together in harmony such different people as the peasant and the writer. Indeed, one could say that the *Encyclopedia* is the utopian projection of such a harmonious order. Likewise he could envisage a scientific scheme of things which would provide a satisfactory explanation for all human behaviour on materialist principles, and he certainly believed fervently in the need for a natural moral order to guarantee human happiness. But he knew too that all these orders were subject to difficulties and contradictions, that Nature is so all-embracing a term as to provide no firm moral or political foundation, and that the desire for universally valid principles is frustrated by the resistance of the real. Diderot's greatness as a thinker seems to me to lie in the way he holds these different impulses in tension one against the other, neither a rationalist nor an empiricist, but a realist.

7 The true, the good and the beautiful

> My trinity, against which the gates of hell will never prevail:
> the true, which is the father, who engenders the good, which
> is the son, from whom proceeds the beautiful, which is the
> holy spirit.
>
> (*Rameau's Nephew*)

The preceding three chapters have given a view of Diderot as a *philosophe*, a man principally concerned with such matters as the true and the good. It was not always easy for him to reconcile the claims of truth and goodness; the natural order of the world was less in harmony with traditional human ideas of virtue and justice than one might wish, nor was it clear that greater knowledge necessarily produced greater goodness and happiness. But the issue was further complicated by the third member of Diderot's trinity, beauty, whose relation to the other two was more problematic than Rameau's confident statement suggests. For the editor of the *Encyclopedia* was also an artist in words, and one who all his life was concerned with art, its values and its function. His thinking about aesthetic matters and his own creative endeavour criss-cross in a fascinating way with his general efforts to make sense of the world and man's place in it.

As a philosopher he had of course to confront the time-honoured questions about the nature of beauty. Is it an unchanging essence to which all human beings can respond, or is it in the eye of the beholder? We have seen in chapter 5 that the desire for unity and order which Diderot shared with most thinkers of his time (and indeed other times) led him to formulate in the *Encyclopedia* article 'Beauty' a rather unsatisfactory theory of beauty, based on 'relationships' – so all-embracing as to be unhelpful in practice. In his later writing on the subject, he tends rather to look for a definition of beauty in the imitation of nature. But this too is by no means a simple notion. As Jacques Chouillet puts it, in his important book *La Formation des idées esthétiques de Diderot* (pp. 390–403), the tension in his aesthetics reflects a clash of two opposed views of nature. The traditional view sees nature as 'firstly a principle of truth and secondly a model to be imitated' – though it is not clear 'whether this model is Nature herself or Nature purified by the mind of man'. The second view, which also had ancient roots but acquired a new lease of life in the eighteenth century, is that of nature as a 'perpetual flux' – as we see it in *D'Alembert's Dream*. Depending on one's concept of nature (and Diderot's is far from stable), the imitation of nature can tend towards idealism (the imitation of 'beautiful nature') or realism (the imitation of ordinary nature, or indeed of nature red in tooth and claw).

One thing is clear however, which is that for Diderot simple imitation of reality was not enough. Beauty also demanded some 'rare and striking circumstance' (E 736), an element of grandeur, approaching what was known in the eighteenth century as the 'sublime'. Whether this sprang from an idealised model of nature and humanity or from the perception of great inhuman forces, Diderot always looked in art for the qualities that astonish and exalt the reader, listener or spectator. There are many words he uses to evoke these qualities, words such as warmth (*chaleur*), verve or poetry. The essential thing is always the powerful effect produced by the work of art. 'Move, me, astonish me, rend me; make me shudder, weep, tremble; fill me with indignation', he apostrophises the

artist in one of his most interesting aesthetic writings, the
Essays on Painting of 1766 (E 714). It was the lack of such
power that he deplored in the art of his day, an art enfeebled
by the progress of civilisation. Rameau speaks for Diderot
when he defends the new Italian music (the operas of
Pergolese, for instance) which allows one to hear 'the animal
cry of passion' and when he mocks the artificiality of French
music.

Against the mannerisms of modern French art, Diderot
often harks back to the sublime grandeur of Homer, the Greek
tragedians and the oratory, sculpture and architecture of
antiquity. His idea of the sublime is a traditional one, and the
insistence on powerful effects reads like a continuation of the
lessons of ancient rhetoric – indeed the very terms used by
Rameau to describe a moving aria (peroration, suspension,
etc.) are taken from this much abused discipline. But at the
same time, Diderot's advocacy of grandeur often leads him to
formulations which with hindsight could be called romantic.
Homer and the Ancients were beginning to appear in a new
light in the eighteenth century: no longer simply schoolroom
models of excellence, they were seen as possessing the power
of the primitive. In his *Discourse on Dramatic Poetry*, Diderot
writes that 'poetry needs something enormous, barbarous and
savage' (E 261), and in the *Essays on Painting* that 'the
imitative arts require something savage, uncultivated, striking and enormous' (E 714). So some of his visions of beauty
have a wild ring to them. Citing an image from a recently
translated Scandinavian poem, he declares in a letter to
Sophie Volland of October 1762:

Powerful effects always come from a mixture of the voluptuous and
the terrible; for instance beautiful half-naked women offering us deli-
cious potions in the bloody skulls of our enemies. That is the model
for everything that is sublime. It is subjects like that which make the
soul melt with pleasure and shudder with fear. (C IV 196)

91

Here, as elsewhere, Diderot's love of the sublime leads him close to the borders of the melodramatic, and his own writing sometimes seems to a modern taste to have gone over the line. His novel *The Nun* is full of excessively vivid scenes of cruelty and vice and piles up horrors in a way that strains our suspension of disbelief (see above, p. 38). And there are moments in almost all of Diderot's fictional and dramatic writings, and indeed in many of his other works, where the eloquence runs too high and the modern reader is likely to feel embarrassed or amused. Diderot may have been moved as he wrote, but the impassioned style with its exclamations, repetitions, accumulations of verbs and monotonously strong vocabulary fails to carry conviction. This tendency to bombast can perhaps be seen as the obverse to one of his most attractive features, the enthusiasm and generosity of feeling which allowed him to respond so fully and warmly to real and imagined experience. The word he used for this is *sensibility*, and in his writings he often returns to the discussion of its place in life and artistic creation.

In the early works sensibility is given the highest possible valuation. Not only is it the quality which makes us moral beings, good friends or loving parents, it is also associated with genius. The genius is seen here as one who is carried away by the intensity of his feelings, like the character Dorval at the beginning of the second of the *Conversations about 'The Natural Son'*:

He had given himself over to the spectacle of nature. His chest was dilated. He was breathing deeply. I could follow in his face the various impressions which he received, and I was beginning to share his enthusiasms as I cried almost unwittingly: 'He is under the spell'. (E 97)

But this figure of genius is all too like the alienated figure whom we see in *Rameau's Nephew*, and in his later writings

Diderot came to have doubts about the relations between sensibility and genius. Aware perhaps of his own excessive emotivity and his relative failure to create great works of art, he now associated genius above all with clear-sighted and detached mastery. This is the view put forward in an extreme form in Diderot's controversial dialogue *The Paradox of the Actor* (the paradox being that the great actor, rather than identifying emotionally with the character, must be devoid of sensibility). The same idea figures in *D'Alembert's Dream*, where Bordeu compares the 'sensitive being', who is at the mercy of his emotivity, to the 'great man', who can control himself and those around him. In the *Essays on Painting*, speaking of the ideal painter, Diderot takes a more balanced view – and quite a classical one – when he speaks of the need for a miraculous combination of enthusiasm and judgement: 'without this perfect equilibrium, according to whether enthusiasm or reason is predominant, the artist is either extravagant or frigid' (E 720).

Such are some of the variations in his views on the qualities which go to the production of works of art. Starting from something like the 'spontaneous overflow of powerful feeling', he arrives at a more Olympian view of the creative process. Interesting as these speculations may be, however, they are perhaps of secondary importance, since what matters most is the *function* of works of art rather than the process by which they are produced. And for Diderot the essential thing is that great works cannot be merely the object of calm appreciation. They must produce strong emotion.

The question then is the old Platonic one: what relation is there between these strong and pleasurable emotions and those primordial values of the *philosophe*, truth and virtue? In his attempts to answer – or exorcise – this question, Diderot returns with obsessive regularity to the image of the trinity

Diderot

which is quoted at the head of this chapter. But the very fact that he insists so often on the indissoluble bond which links the three persons of this trinity might alert us to its fragility. Let us consider in turn the relations of beauty to truth and to goodness.

As far as truth is concerned, the notion of the imitation of nature would suggest that when we are stirred by a painting or a play, this is because the artist has given a faithful rendering of a stirring scene. In describing paintings in his *Salons*, Diderot often seems to enter the canvas, walk around in it and discuss its images as if they were the real thing. In the theatre and fiction too he looks for a lifelike rendering of the world. This is what he finds in his idol Richardson:

The world in which we live is his scene; his drama is based on truth; his characters are utterly real and are taken from the midst of society . . . the trials and tribulations of his characters are of the kind which threaten me at any time; he shows me the general order of things which surrounds me. (E 30–1)

Such truthfulness, adds Diderot, is a necessary condition for the moral working of art.

Obviously, this begs a great many questions. In the first place, can all the arts be described in terms of the imitation of reality? What of architecture? What of music? And even when there is an element of imitation involved, we may doubt whether the effectiveness of the work depends as much as Diderot suggests on the truthfulness of the rendering. Do not falsity, exaggeration and fantasy also affect us? Perhaps Diderot would have liked to answer 'no' to this question; so one gathers from an interesting discussion of Greuze in the *Salon* of 1765. But as a writer of plays and fiction he knew from experience that the medium of literature is not transparent, that if art creates an illusion of truth, it also deforms, exaggerates and deceives – and we like to be deceived. One of the places where this is most clearly recognised is in the concluding paragraphs of *The Two Friends of Bourbonne*, a story of noble devotion among peasants, smugglers and charcoal-burners. In my view this story fails as a realistic imitation of nature (though it succeeds in other ways) because of Diderot's 'sublime' eloquence as story-teller and creator of dialogue. At the end of the story, however, comes a most interesting discussion of realism in literature. Leaving on one side the accepted unreality of heroic and comic narration, Diderot poses the problem of the 'historic' (i.e. realistic) story-teller. He must be believed if his story is to have its effect, but equally he must tell a story which goes beyond the limits of normality – otherwise we should not bother to listen. He had to reconcile truth, or the appearance of truth, with what Diderot calls 'poetry' (a term used equally of painting to describe the sublime conceptions which are needed for the creation of a moving picture of human life). The solution that Diderot proposed (the addition of warts to an ideal face) does not perhaps take one very far, but it is fascinating to see him wrestling with the divergent demands of art and truthfulness.

It is the same with painting. His inclination, as we have seen, is towards the grand and the sublime, which means for instance the seascapes of Vernet (above all scenes of storm and shipwreck), the eloquent domestic scenes of Greuze, or the great tableaux from mythology or history which dominated the art of the time. But he also has an intense admiration for the truthfulness of Chardin's still-life paintings, irrespective of the subject-matter, and marvels at the illusion of light, texture, space and air: 'It is nature itself; the objects stand out from the canvas with a truth which deceives the eye' (E 483).

Chardin is perhaps the exception that proves the rule. On the whole the *Salons* and the *Essays on Painting* give the impression that Diderot's real preference goes to those he calls history painters, those whose paintings tell stirring stories. The history painter is a 'poet', who works in the world of great ideas, whereas the still-life painter is a 'philosopher', attentive above all to the real. Ideally, as in the *Thoughts on the Interpretation of Nature*, patient attention should be married to imaginative sweep. But in any case, the reproduction of reality in a still life leaves room for an element of 'magic'. Both Chardin and Vernet are *creators* and are compared to God in the *Salons*. In a phrase that prefigures the aesthetics of romanticism, Diderot writes that 'the painter's sun is not and cannot be the sun of the universe' (E 600). Truth to life is neither possible nor sufficient.

The problem of art and truth is posed in a different form when the production of an artistic effect is seen to rely not merely on imaginative transfiguration, but on a false view of the world, a fantasy or a myth. As a rationalist, Diderot was conscious of the oddity in our continued use of mythological subjects. He wrote in the *Salon* of 1765: 'I will not blush to confess that Greuze's *Betrothal* interests me more than the *Judgement of Paris*' (A X 278). *A fortiori* he looked askance at the childishness of the story of Blue Beard (E 156). But atheist or not, he could also see that what he called the 'abominable cross' was a great source of moving subjects for art and literature. Writing to Grimm in the *Salon* of 1765 about the powerful effect of the Corpus Christi processions even on a nonbeliever, he admits that 'there is in it something grand, sombre, solemn and melancholy' (compare the sentences on poetry and arts quoted above, p. 91). And he concludes, with teasing ambiguity: 'My friend, if we prefer truth to art, let us ask God for iconoclasts' (A X 391).

Now it can be argued (indeed it seems obvious) that a painting of, say, the Annunciation or the Birth of Venus does not require us to believe in the truth of the religious system it embodies, and that dreams, fantasies and myths also have a truth to tell about and for humanity. Nor is there any need to accept the ideology of sainthood and martyrdom to be moved (as Diderot certainly was) by the human drama of many stories from early Church history. But at the very least one must speak of a split in his reactions here. On the one hand, the desire for a truth stripped clean of all illusions; on the other hand, the emotional need for an art which seemed bound to embellish, exaggerate and falsify. No doubt this split expresses itself in his own ironic practice as a writer.

What now of the relation between beauty and goodness? For Diderot there was, or ought to be, a clear connection between moral and aesthetic values. Discussing human beauty in the *Essays on Painting*, he declares:

Consider your reaction to the appearance of a man or a woman, and you will recognise that what attracts or repels you is always the image of a good quality or the obvious or not so obvious sign of a bad one. (E 697)

He goes on, it is true, to admit that different individuals or groups have different moral preferences and therefore different moral tastes. A man of eighteen will like a certain sort of female beauty, whereas a man of fifty will have a different perspective on things. But this does not open the door to the relativism which Diderot feared:

Who has good taste? Is it myself at eighteen or myself at fifty? It is easy to decide. If I had been asked at eighteen: 'My boy, which is the more beautiful, the image of vice or the image of virtue?' I should have answered: 'What a question! The image of virtue'. (E 698)

Given this sort of security, Diderot is very severe on the immoral art of Boucher. On the other hand, he is bowled over by the work of Greuze, in whom he sees a perfect combination

97

of truthfulness (Greuze paints from real, ordinary life), goodness (Greuze's paintings are sermons in print) and therefore
beauty. Because these paintings are so remote from present
taste, it is hard for us to recapture the enthusiasm they aroused
in Diderot. They were for him what we now call 'committed'
art; he saw in them not only true representations of reality but
speaking images of the reward of virtue and the punishment of
vice. The *Beloved Mother*, for instance, a genre painting which
would strike most modern spectators as both funny and
ambivalent, provokes this comment:

It is excellent, both for talent and for morals. It preaches in favour of
population, and it gives a most moving picture of the inestimable
happiness and value of domestic harmony. It says to any man of
feeling and good sense: 'Keep your family in comfort, give your wife
children, as many as you can; be faithful to her, and you can be sure of
being happy in your home.' (E 546)

Greuze, he says repeatedly, is *his* painter; in his moralising
painting he sees the equivalent of his own efforts in the theatre:
'should we not be satisfied to see the brush at last joining
forces with dramatic poetry to move us, educate us, improve
us and inspire us to virtue?' (E 524).

These views, and the eloquence that goes with them, have
not worn well; this is the face of Diderot that is hardest to
accept, but it is none the less real for all that. It is true that as
time went by he acquired a greater sense of the painterly
qualities of painting. Chardin and Vernet came to occupy a
more central place in his contemporary pantheon, and there
was a certain cooling towards Greuze. But the idea of a moral
art never left him.

On the other hand, for all the apparent confidence of the
passages from the *Essays on Painting* about the moral basis of
aesthetic judgement, Diderot knew very well that there are

kinds of beauty very different from the virtuous art of Greuze. Among the figures of sublimity are not only the heroes of Corneille's tragedies or the God of the Book of Genesis, but also the great and alarming forces of nature, the whirlwinds and the volcanoes. So Diderot reacts with his usual enthusiasm to the images of storm and shipwreck offered by Vernet; undeserved and violent death is a source of beauty here. And then there are the human equivalents of the volcano or the storm, great criminals who bring suffering to humanity. They too can be beautiful. It will be remembered that in *Rameau's Nephew* Rameau shocks the philosopher by presenting for his admiration a piece of consummate villainy. 'Myself' refuses to confuse moral and aesthetic judgement in this way, but Diderot's writing shows time and again how conscious he was of the aesthetic appeal of crime, both in life and in art.

There are several moral arguments advanced by Diderot for the depiction of evil in art. For one thing, as in melodrama, the spectacle of crime arouses sympathy for the victims, and this sort of sympathy is supposed to be morally improving. Or again, it can be argued that we learn to hate evil by seeing it vividly represented with all its consequences. But this, like the previous argument, falls foul of Diderot's obvious admiration for the great criminal. Even in Richardson's *Clarissa*, improving though it may be, there is for him a sort of fascination in the villainy of Lovelace. This is exacerbated in the case of the great criminals of history and legend, Clytemnestra, Tarquin or Caligula. What Diderot responds to here, as in the spectacle of inanimate nature, is sheer energy. From the very early *Philosophical Thoughts* he had sung the praises of the passions: 'only the passions, and the great passions, can elevate the soul to great things.' Later on, many times, he came back to the praise of such exceptional beings as the would-be regicide Damiens, who faced his terrible sentence with a sang-froid that overwhelmed the sensitive *philosophe*. Such sublimity goes beyond good and evil, and Diderot can only bring this into line with his desire to moralise by claiming, as he does more than once, that

If the wicked did not show this energy in the cause of evil, the virtuous would not show it in the cause of good. If debilitated man has lost the strength to commit great crimes, he will have no strength for great acts of virtue. In seeking to improve him in one way, you will degrade him in others. If Tarquin no longer dares to violate Lucretia, Scaevola will not hold out his wrist over the burning coals. (C III 98)

So great crime is preferable to mediocre virtue, even in life, and how much more so in art, feeding as it does on our love of the exceptional.

If we attempt now to summarise Diderot's ideas about art, we can see that his thinking oscillates between opposite poles as well as developing over time. There are moments, as in all his works, where he throws out brilliant anticipations of later ideas. His main virtue, as always, is not so much to lay out a coherent theory of the nature of beauty or genius or the relations between art and truth or morality, but to come at such questions from many angles, apparently contradicting himself at times, but bringing to the discussion both a philosophically enquiring mind and considerable practical knowledge. His dominant conception of art is as an activity which gains its human value from its powerful and moving representations of those aspects of nature which most concern us, and his ideal art (however hard to realise in practice) is one in which this emotional response is in harmony with his philosophical values of truth and goodness.

These are fine sentiments, and Diderot is always interesting, if not always entirely convincing, in what he writes about the various arts. But he also had aspirations to be not just a *philosophe* but a creative writer, the author of the *belle page* which he was inclined to put on a level with the *belle action*. What then of his own work as an artist? How does it square with his aesthetic ideas? In what ways does it remain significant and valuable?

It must be said immediately that Diderot was not very successful in producing the kind of art he apparently most admired. This is not to say that his writing lacks vitality. On the contrary, one feels the constant pulsing of adventure and excitement in his dialogues, his philosophical writing, his story-telling and even his *Encyclopedia* articles. He is a master in the vivid and rapid expression of a scene, a mood or a thought, but one does not often find in his work the sublime and unequivocal representation of passion and energy that he admired in Homer, Richardson or Vernet. It is true that there are a few works which aim to create a sustained effect of pathos, notably the two plays of the 1750s and perhaps *The Nun* and *The Two Friends of Bourbonne*. The plays are among their author's least successful writings, and I think we can be grateful that he never completed a drama entitled *The Sheriff*, which was conceived as a modern equivalent of ancient tragedy, an excessively black and white melodrama. Perhaps it is significant that he did not manage to complete this work; he was not single-minded enough to be a modern Sophocles.

As for the fiction, it should be remembered that the moving if exaggerated story-telling of *The Nun* and *The Two Friends* is not allowed to stand on its own. Both works were hoaxes, and Diderot does not allow the reader to forget this, accompanying the central text with explanatory material which, like the notes to *The Waste Land*, casts an ironic light on the narrative. It is the same with almost all of his eloquent passages; they must be read in context. The thrilling speculations about the

101

evolution of the world in *D'Alembert's Dream* are framed by sensible and often light-hearted conversation; the classical harangue of the old man in the *Supplement to Bougainville's Voyage* is made the object of detached and quizzical discussion; the hymn to sexuality in the *Encyclopedia* article 'Pleasure' (*Jouissance*) takes its place between Jovinianism (a heretical Christian sect) and Day (*Jour*), while the denunciations of colonialism which Diderot contributed to Raynal's *History of The Two Indies* are inserted into a large and not always very exciting patchwork of a book. In all these cases we have a brief or not so brief passage of eloquence which is set against other, contrasting elements. The one does not negate the other; both have to be taken into account.

A common experience in reading Diderot is one of discontinuity. It is odd therefore that in his writing about art he should have been so insistent on unity. It is in the name of unity that, like a true French classicist, he condemns the tasteless mixture of tones in Shakespeare. In the *Discourse on Dramatic Poetry* he affirms that 'nothing is beautiful if it is not unified', and condemns artists who work in contrasts (E 234–5). And in his writing about painting we find a similar taste for works whose strong effect is due to the simplicity, clarity and unity of their subject and manner; in a very unmodern way he declares: 'I want my pleasure to be pure and effortless; I turn my back on the painter who presents me with an emblem or a riddle to decipher'. It is true that he immediately goes on to demand 'variety', but this variety remains subordinate to the controlling influence of the artist's central idea.

Now it is true that painting and writing make different demands on the artist; a picture is seen all at once, whereas a book is experienced over time. (A similar comparison might be made between plays and novels.) It is also true that 'unity' is an elastic concept; with effort one can unearth a unity in almost any work. Certainly there has been no lack of attempts to find the centre or 'secret chain' in such apparently chaotic creations as *Jacques the Fatalist* or *Rameau's Nephew* – which are indeed unified by the constant presence of their author, his major concerns, his favourite themes, images and words, the rhythms of his prose. But it would be stretching terms to see in them an exemplification of the more traditional sort of unity he favoured in his aesthetic theories. As an art critic Diderot may prefigure romantic attitudes, but he is an 'ancient' in his strong admiration for what Schiller called the 'naïve'; as a writer however he is a 'modern', varied, ironical and contradictory. He is also a *comic* writer, and comedy too is something which does not figure prominently in his writing about art. All of these qualities may be seen in the work of his maturity which perhaps best exhibits his peculiar qualities as a writer, *Jacques the Fatalist*.

Probably the best way to give an idea of the nature of Diderot's novel (or anti-novel) is to allow it to speak for itself. Here is the opening:

How had they met? By chance, like everyone else. What were their names? What's that to you? Where had they come from? The last place along the road. Where were they going? Does anyone know where he is going? What were they saying? The master was saying nothing and Jacques was saying that his captain used to say that all the good and evil that befalls us on earth was already written in the Book of Destiny.

MASTER. That's a weighty saying for you.

JACQUES. My captain also used to say that every bullet has its billet.

MASTER. And quite right he was too.

'Damn that innkeeper and his inn!' exclaimed Jacques after a short pause.

MASTER. What are you damning your neighbour for? It's not
Christian.

JACQUES. I'll tell you: I get drunk on his filthy wine and forget to
water the horses. My father finds out; he gets cross. I shrug my
shoulders; he picks up a stick and gives my back a bit of a tickling.
A regiment is passing on its way to Fontenoy; in a fit of temper I
enlist. We reach camp; battle is joined.

MASTER. And you received the bullet destined for you.

JACQUES. Exactly. Shot in the knee I was, and God knows what
good and bad fortune that bullet has brought me. It all hangs
together just like the links of a chain. If it hadn't been for that
bullet for instance, I don't suppose I should ever have been in love,
or lame either.

MASTER. So you have been in love, Jacques?

JACQUES. Have I been in love!

MASTER. And all because of a bullet?

JACQUES. All because of a bullet.

MASTER. You never said a word about it before.

JACQUES. I should think not!

MASTER. Why not?

JACQUES. Because there was an appointed time for telling the tale.

MASTER. And has that time come?

JACQUES. Who knows?

MASTER. Well, go ahead, anyway . . .

Jacques began his tale of love. It was the afternoon; the weather was
sultry; his master went to sleep. At nightfall they were still far from
shelter. So there they are, quite lost, and the master in a tearing rage
thrashing his valet with his whip, and the poor wretch saying at every
stroke: 'I suppose that one was written in the Book too . . .'

As you see, dear reader, I am well away, and if I wanted to, I could
make you wait a year or two, or even three, for Jacques's love story,
simply by separating him from his master and dragging each of them
through all the adventures I chose to invent. What's to stop me

marrying off the master and cuckolding him? Or shipping Jacques off to the Indies, sending his master after him and bringing them both back to France on the same boat? How easy it is to tell stories! (R 521–3)

Those who know *Tristram Shandy* can see where Diderot got his starting point, but his spare and rapid manner is very different from Sterne's luxuriant style. Here already we can see the two framing dialogues of the novel (author–reader, Jacques–master). The travels of the latter couple are set in motion, but also the story of Jacques's 'loves'. Both of these will wind their way through the whole novel, neither reaching any clear conclusion. The first of many brief scenes from everyday life is sketched, and two of the major themes of the novel are broached: the teasing questions of fatalism and of the novelist's art and truth. And equally, the image of the links of a chain nudges us to think about the connections between all the stories and conversations we are about to read.

The stories are many and various, ranging from inconsequential little anecdotes to the fully developed history of Madame de la Pommeraye and the marquis des Arcis. This is a tale of the long-planned vengeance of a woman who has been rejected by her lover; it is full of physical and psychological detail and the dialogue comes across with greater liveliness than that of Diderot's plays. Taken by itself it makes a powerful and realistic work. Indeed readers from Schiller onwards have been tempted to extract it from *Jacques* and treat it in isolation. But the point is that in the novel the story is told by the hostess of an inn to Jacques and his master, and told with an incredible number of interruptions (which the author added to, as was his habit, with successive versions of the book). What is more, the interruptions include not only calls from the other travellers in the inn, but comments from story-teller and listeners and the retailing of little anecdotes or

105

fables in a quite different tonality from that of the tale of vengeance. Here for instance is a passage in which the marquis has found out that Madame de la Pommeraye has tricked him into marrying a prostitute:

The poor creature remained lying in the same position and made no reply. The marquis was sitting in an armchair, his head wrapped in his arms and his body half leaning against the foot of his bed, not looking at her, but shouting from time to time: 'Go away.' The silence and immobility of the unfortunate woman surprised him; he repeated in an even louder voice: 'Will you go away; can't you hear me?' Then he bent down, pushed her away roughly, and finding that she was unconscious and almost lifeless, picked her up by the middle of the body, laid her on a sofa, and looked at her for a moment with eyes in which anger alternated with commiseration. (R 573)

The narrator here is the hostess, and her hearers comment on her unexpected skill and eloquence. At this point, towards the climax of her story, she is talking almost without interruption, but earlier on Jacques had helped fill a gap in the story with such things as the fable of the knife and the sheath. This too is about marital fidelity, but its style is very different:

One day the sheath and the knife had a quarrel. The knife said to the sheath: 'Sheath, my friend, you are a wicked woman, for every day you take in new knives'. The sheath replied to the knife: 'Knife, my friend, you are a wicked man, for every day you change sheaths . . .' (R 633)

This is a very obvious contrast – between these two poles the novel contains a great range of different voices, corresponding to a host of different people and scenes. And all the time, giving a sort of unity to this labyrinthine and many-faceted work, there is the voice of the author, who is at once the god who controls this little world, the scribe who records the real universe in its puzzling and amusing complexity, and the writer who as he writes, parodies, criticises, discusses and praises the many other attempts to write down the world in fiction. *Jacques* is a novel which prefigures the modern novel in its highlighting of the codes of writing.

There are Greuze-like scenes in all this (though very little of Chardin or Vernet), but the total effect is as unlike Greuze as could be imagined. It is a novel full of life, but above all an *intelligent* novel, asking its reader to take part in a game of words – a game which struck Goethe on his first reading as a feast worthy of Baal. And in this respect there is no distinction to be made between Diderot's fiction and the rest of his writing. One does not go to him for a great illumination. If (in the words of the Russian proverb cited by Isaiah Berlin in his study of Tolstoy) the fox knows many things, but the hedgehog knows one big thing, then Diderot, for all his aspiration to unity, was not a hedgehog. Perhaps, like Tolstoy, he was a fox who wanted to be a hedgehog, but the real hedgehog was his friend, later his enemy, Jean-Jacques Rousseau, a man with a message, who still speaks to readers with a greater intensity than we find in Diderot. Nor was he a poet; one looks in vain in his work for the sublimity that he himself found in Vernet or Homer and that we may find in Wordsworth or Pushkin. No, both in historical terms and in his continuing impact today, Diderot's value seems to me to lie in his excited and exciting openness to the world, his anticipations of the new, his humour, his diversity. I am not sure that he is best described as a 'past master', but he is a supremely *interesting* writer.

Further reading

Writings by Diderot

The standard *Œuvres complètes*, edited by J. Assézat and M. Tourneux (20 vols, Paris, 1875-7) is now being superseded by the new *Œuvres complètes*, edited by numerous specialists under the direction of H. Dieckmann, J. Proust and J. Varloot (Paris, 1975-). This will be the scholarly edition for the foreseeable future. An attractive reading edition of the complete works is that of R. Lewinter (15 vols, Paris, Club Français du Livre, 1969-73). For easier access, much of Diderot's main work is contained in four volumes in the Classiques Garnier series: *Œuvres philosophiques*, edited by P. Vernière (Paris, 1956), *Œuvres esthétiques*, edited by P. Vernière (Paris, 1959), *Œuvres politiques*, edited by P. Vernière (Paris, 1963) and *Œuvres romanesques*, edited by H. Bénac, revised by L. Perol (Paris, 1981). Other important French-language editions include the *Salons*, edited by J. Seznec and J. Adhémar (4 vols, Oxford, 1957-67) and the *Correspondance*, edited by G. Roth and J. Varloot (16 vols, Paris, 1955-70).

The original edition of the *Encyclopédie* is available in many major libraries; a good selection from it is that by J. Lough, *The Encyclopédie of Diderot and D'Alembert* (Cambridge, 1954).

Diderot's writings are not easy to obtain in English translation. The following have appeared relatively recently:

Rameau's Nephew and Other Works, translated by J. Barzun (Indianapolis, 1964).

Rameau's Nephew and *D'Alembert's Dream*, translated by L. Tancock (Harmondsworth, 1966).

The Nun, translated by L. Tancock (Harmondsworth, 1974).

Jacques the Fatalist and his Master, translated by J. R. Loy (New York, 1959).

Selections from the Encyclopaedia, translated by S. J. Gendzier (New York, 1959).

Letters to Sophie Volland, translated by P. France (London, 1972). There is also a good new anthology, with introductory comments and sizeable extracts in translation from many different works, *The Irresistible Diderot* by J. Hope Mason (London, 1982).

Writings about Diderot

The best biography of Diderot is the monumental work of A. M. Wilson, *Diderot* (New York, 1972). Of short introductions in French the best is probably that of J. Chouillet, *Diderot* (Paris, 1977), but the older illustrated essay by C. Guyot, *Diderot par lui-même* (Paris, 1965) can also be recommended, as can the stimulating lectures by H. Dieckmann, *Cinq leçons sur Diderot* (Paris, 1959). In English a good brief introduction is provided by the chapter on Diderot in R. Niklaus, *A Literary History of France, the Eighteenth Century* (London, 1970), and a fuller view by L. G. Crocker, *Diderot's Chaotic Order*, which places him in a context of thought and feeling portrayed at greater length in the same author's *An Age of Crisis* (Baltimore, 1959) and *Nature and Culture* (Baltimore, 1963). For a nineteenth-century English view which has worn well, see John Morley, *Diderot and the Encyclopedists* (2 vols, London, 1878).

There are many interesting short general essays devoted to Diderot. I have found the following particularly worthwhile: M. Butor, 'Diderot le fataliste et ses maîtres' in his *Répertoire III* (Paris, 1968); J. Starobinski, 'Diderot et la parole des autres', *Critique*, 28 (1972), pp. 3–22; L. Trilling, *Sincerity and Authenticity* (Oxford, 1972), Chapter 2; and several of the articles gathered together in J. Proust, *L'Objet et le texte* (Geneva, 1980). Thomas Carlyle's 'Diderot' (1833), reprinted in his *Critical and Miscellaneous Essays*, is still worth reading for its hostile, supercilious, yet in its way perceptive reaction to all the *philosophe* stood for.

On Diderot the writer see R. Lewinter, *Diderot, ou les mots de l'absence* (Paris, 1976); G. May, 'Diderot, artiste et philosophe du décousu', in *Europäische Aufklärung*, edited by H. Friedrich and F. Schalk (Munich, 1976); J. Undank, *Diderot, Inside, Outside and In-Between* (Madison, 1979); and P. France, *Rhetoric and Truth in France* (Oxford, 1972), Chapter 6.

Diderot

The scientific problems of *D'Alembert's Dream* and related works are discussed in A. Vartanian, *Diderot and Descartes* (Princeton, 1953); J. Roger, *Les Sciences de la vie dans la pensée française du XVIIIe siècle* (Paris, 1963), Part III, Chapter 3; Emita B. Hill, 'The Role of "le Monstre" in Diderot's Thought', *Studies on Voltaire and the Eighteenth Century*, 97 (1972), pp. 147–261; and 'Studies on the Rêve de d'Alembert' (by various hands) *Diderot Studies*, 17 (1973), pp. 13–106.

The best work on the *Encyclopédie* is that of J. Proust, *Diderot et l'Encyclopédie* (Paris, 1962) which is an impressively wide-ranging study. Proust has also written a short introductory work, *L'Encyclopédie* (Paris, 1965).

Helpful discussions of Diderot's political and social thought will be found in A. Strugnell, *Diderot's Politics* (The Hague, 1973) and Y. Benot *Diderot, de l'athéisme à l'anti-colonialisme* (Paris, 1970), while his interest in non-European peoples is examined in M. Duchet, *Anthropologie et histoire au siècle des lumières* (Paris, 1971), Chapter 5.

Aesthetics has been prominent in Diderot scholarship in recent years. J. Chouillet, *La Formation des idées esthétiques de Diderot, 1743–1763* (Paris, 1973) is a particularly rich and illuminating work. See also M. T. Cartwright, 'Diderot critique d'art et le problème de l'expression', *Diderot Studies*, 13 (1969) and M. Hobson, *The Object of Art* (Cambridge, 1982).

One should also mention writing on Diderot's fiction. On *Jacques* and the novel, there is J. R. Loy, *Diderot's Determined Fatalist* (New York, 1950) and R. Kempf, *Diderot et le roman* (Paris, 1964), which sees him as a precursor of modernist fiction. On *Rameau's Nephew* there is an immense literature: the introduction by Jean Fabre to his edition of this work (Geneva, 1950) is an excellent starting point, and some idea of the differences of opinion about the dialogue can be had from *Entretiens sur le Neveu de Rameau*, edited by M. Launay and M. Duchet (Paris, 1967). There are two valuable studies in English: H. Josephs, *Diderot's Dialogue of Gesture and Language* (Ohio, 1969) and D. O'Gorman, *Diderot the Satirist* (Toronto, 1971).

Further reading

Since 1949 twenty volumes have appeared of the periodical *Diderot Studies*, which carries articles, longer studies and reviews on all kinds of topic. A full bibliography up to the mid 1970s is F. A. Spear, *Bibliographie de Diderot* (Geneva, 1980), and Diderot's changing fortunes are traced in J. Proust, *Lectures de Diderot* (Paris , 1974).

This is a small selection of work directly concerned with the *philosophe*. It goes without saying, however, that a section on further reading should really include works by his contemporaries (above all, Rousseau) and such general studies of the Enlightenment as those of Cassirer, Gay and Hampson. But that would take us beyond the bounds of the present small book.

Index

113

Index

Index

DATE DUE

D0386428